Gur

Jap Meditation Revealed

*Guru Nanak's Revolutionary
Spiritual System*

Gurmeet Singh

Copyright Notice: ©2019 Gurmeet Singh
All Rights Reserved.
No portion of
this material may be transcribed,
photocopied, reproduced or transmitted
in any form, either mechanical or
electronic—including recording or
placing into any information storage
system, computer network or on
the Internet—without prior written
permission from the author.
(only the Japji and the English translation
is free for use on mention of source)
This book is priceless knowledge for spiritual transformation. The price
is a form of donation, which funds further projects.

ISBN:9781099993558

Contents

1. Jap Meditation and Japji — 5
2. Authors Note — 8
3. The Mool Mantar – — 9
4. Pauris from 1 to 38 — 21
5. ਸਲੋਕ ॥ Salok — 108
6. Jap Meditation Explained — 110
7. The Jap and New Age — 118
8. About the Author — 119

1. Jap Meditation and Japji

Guru Nanak's Revolutionary Spiritual System was first revealed in Japji composition. It is a sacred composition by Guru Nanak (1469-1539) and forms a part of Gurbani (word of the Guru). The hymns compiled in the holy scripture bestowed are with Guruship and is known as Guru Granth Sahib. Only these are refered as Gurbani (Guru's Word).

The Gurbani in Guru Granth Sahib, has a pure spiritual emphasis on Sach (truth). This truth is about ultimate reality hidden in the nature of creation. The knowledge of truth *opens up conscious awareness* from ignorance to discernment of true reality as a part of thread in the connected whole.

Japji as a whole begins with the Mool Mantar (Root Mantar), in the beginning. It is a composition of words encompassing the entire universally complex theology describing the ultimate reality and the Jap method of meditation to achieve oneness. The Mool Mantar in Japji is followed by 38 stanzas traditionally called Pauri (steps) and a concluding Salok (couplet).

The reality of creation is hidden. Gurbani calls it Sach, the truth. It's knowledge and awareness come only when we go within away from the flow of thoughts. Our origin is this Sach.

This Book

This book "too" follows the Jap method. The translation is followed by "comments" elaborating upon the translation.

Gurbani words are in poetic style. The brief words signify and indicate the truth. The contemplation on these words is a part of Jap Meditation. This method lets the mind look beyond the Maya-the illusion that hides the true reality.

The state of our "world of form" is real but is not the eternal Sach (truth). The Maya, keeps our mind diverted from following up any process that lets us know the truth. The Vichar (contemplation) on the words in Gurbani then begins to reveal the hidden indications of the true reality.

The *Mool Mantar* is to be read and contemplated again and again. It has depths of underlying meaning and forms the basis of Jap Meditation. The Mool (Root or origin) holds the secret to the real truth.

The Mool is elaborated in Pauris building up the other facets of the Jap. These are to be contemplated. The fast reading means the mind would skip the true meaning.

There is influence of Maya on our mind. It is reflected in its working when there is dullness or thought activity. The Maya diverts mind activity towards the world affairs and attractions.

This activity of Maya is less during early morning known as Amritvela between 3.00AM to 6.00 AM. This is ambrosial hour for contemplation and going within.

This is the time for Jap Meditation.

Gurbani Script

Gurbani is written in Gurmukhi script. For those not conversant with it, the transliteration is given. The recitation of Gurbani can be done with it. The Gurbani is written in poetic style that matches the thought

process and the words can be repeated through singing with music as a form of Jap.

Jap Meditation

The secrets of Jap Meditation are explained after Japji translation.

It is suggested that the whole translation and comments be read first and then return back to comprehend through the process of Jap.

The words used in Gurbani have special significance and do not have correct translation so these are adopted.

The Sach, meaning truth, that the Gurbani talks about is hidden. We cannot perceive it nor experience it through our physical body senses as these are part of creation. Neither can it be perceived through our mind.

The perception is through Sach part only. The conscious awareness is a part of Sach and is eternal. It is part of soul that ever exists. Only *Haume* is created part that we consider as our real self.

2. Authors Note

Religion is a specific set of beliefs or practices usually connected to an organized group. Some people find spirituality by practicing their religious beliefs, while others find it outside of an organized structure.

> *True spirituality is personal. Spiritual life is not in rites or rituals. It begins when we go within. Inside world is formless. There we are at a level similar to that needed to understand Gurbani.*

Gurbani being poetic is self-read and self- listened. It would then pull awareness within. Only then contemplate on "Japji "looking for meaning and indications
beyond the words. The translation is inspired and has a connection. The thoughts open up doors of awareness and knowledge.

 The true guide is met within. For hearing the voice we have to be open first. The inner Guru is formless and imperceptible. The Jap Meditation opens up the Awareness. The first guide is Gurbani which teaches the Jap Meditation.

 The moment perception opens up, the voice is heard. In this age, only Gurbani is needed to find and know God.

3.The Mool Mantar – verse that explains reality

The "Mool Mantar" means the "Root Verse". It tells about the Origin of Creation and the method to know reality.

It is a composition that depicts nature of Creation and removes our ignorance about the Creator, our origin along with the method to live in awareness.

This short verse is here on earth for us. But our state is such that the symbols of success and wealth are more important to us. Most of us are living a life of ignorance. About our present state the Gurbani says:

ਮੂਲੁ ਨ ਬੁਝੈ ਆਪੁ ਨ ਸੁਝੈ ਭਰਮਿ ਬਿਆਪੀ ਅਹੰ ਮਨੀ ॥੧॥

We do not try to comprehend the origin so the self remains not known; as there prevails misconception and egotism in mind. (Guru Granth Sahib: 1186).

The Mool Mantar speaks of the ultimate truth and the secret of finding it is summed up in this composition.

The Mool Mantar is not a chant as some take it to be so. It is to be understood by way of contemplation. For the revelations to uncover we have to repeatedly look at the words and their significance again and again. This method is of Jap. The Jap lets us mold our mind to accept the reality not yet visible or experienced.

This composition of Japji that comes after this verse is knowledge that lets our mind believe rather develop faith.

These words are also mystic in nature and cannot be easily translated.

Below through a brief description the indicated meaning is

given. These words are new concepts but it is pertinent to mention that the Mool Mantar is not a one time reading.

The meaning connected with meditation are explained further in the chapter.

The Mool Mantar is as below:

ੴ Ikongkaar
There is Oneness.
From ONE origin, has formed All creation.
Wherein resounds the celestial sound of creation.

ਸਤਿ ਨਾਮੁ Satnaam
The only truth in creation is the Naam- that signifies formless, eternal, unseen hidden presence of the ONE.

ਕਰਤਾ ਪੁਰਖੁ Karta Purakh
In the creation is the all-encompassing presence of the ONE as Purakh, who is the Karta (doer). The Hukam (command) creates and makes creation function.

ਨਿਰਭਉ Nirbhau
The fear is not a part of the true ONE.

ਨਿਰਵੈਰੁ Nirvair
The ONE is ever immaculate, with no enmity.

ਅਕਾਲ ਮੂਰਤਿ Akal Moorat
The all that is, the reality that is the truth is eternal- is without death and time.

ਅਜੂਨੀ Ajooni
The ONE is all there is, is not any species.

ਸੈਭੰ Saibhang
The true one, is all that there is self- created.

ਗੁਰ ਪ੍ਰਸਾਦਿ **Gurprasadh**

The ONE is known through the Guru - the true guide within. The Prashad is return gift from the Guru.

॥ ਜਪੁ ॥ **Jap**

To Know and Meet. Meditate the Jap way.
(Jap is to identify by repeating, keeping focus on the Sach, the True ONE whose presence is Naam as indicated in the Mool Mantar).

ਆਦਿ ਸਚੁ ਜੁਗਾਦਿ ਸਚੁ ॥ ਹੈ ਭੀ ਸਚੁ ਨਾਨਕ ਹੋਸੀ ਭੀ ਸਚੁ ॥੧॥
Aadh Sach Jugaadh Sach. Hai Bhee Sach Nanak Hosee Bhee Sach.

The True ONE existed before any beginning, True ONE exists thereafter, True ONE is present in now and, says Nanak, True ONE shall remain existing in the future.

Comments:

The Gurbani, itself describes Mool Mantar in the line:

ਮੂਲ ਮੰਤ੍ਰੁ ਹਰਿ ਨਾਮੁ ਰਸਾਇਣੁ ਕਹੁ ਨਾਨਕ ਪੂਰਾ ਪਾਇਆ ॥

The Mool Mantar, is the essence of *Har Naam* (Lord Master's quality), says Nanak, that brings completeness with finding of the origin. *(Guru Granth Sahib: 1040).*

Har word is frequently used in Gurbani to signify the aspect of the true ONE, an endearing loving feeling. The Naam is a single word which is the representation of the truth intermingled in the duality of creation.

The beginning word ੴ Ikongkaar is representative with indications leading towards a higher level which is understood only by experience.

Gurmeet Singh

The number One here signifying the singularity of origingives rise to form. This singularity is reflected in the name- Ekankar as mentioned in Gurbani, the Guru's hymns.

Science too has reached a level where this is part of the proposed understanding of mathametical equations. Scientist Stephan Hawkins has put forward this view.
Th Gurbani explains it that the Creation does not exist or is present in the Nirankar (formless) state of Sunn Samadhi state assumed by the Creator. The creation as we know does not exist there. In the creation are material forms. The non-material part of creation are the emotions, thoughts, social structure, laws . It has our personality, past, present, future and linear time flow.
In the figure 1 is shown Creation flow.

At the level of *Sunn* there is nothing. None of the above exist. Absolutly no creation. The only everexisting is the Ekankar which is present in creation but is not within our perception. This essence is like presence of fragerance in a flower. The Guru calls this presence as Sach, the unchanging, everexisting as is the truth. The creation whereas is transcient, has polarity defining it, cyclic in nature. Its main feature is non-permanence.

How to know this imperceptible Sach, the truth is the first revelation of the Mool Mantar. Next is where the true one resides. The Gurbani initially answers it by apprising that the Ekankar is here within and everywhere a singular infinite ever existence and presence.

In the hymn on page 250 the Guru says:

ਆਦਿ ਮਧਿ ਅੰਤਿ ਨਿਰੰਕਾਰੰ ॥ ਆਪਹਿ ਸੁੰਨ ਆਪਹਿ ਸੁਖ ਆਸਨ ॥
ਆਪਹਿ ਸੁਨਤ ਆਪ ਹੀ ਜਾਸਨ ॥ ਆਪਨ ਆਪੁ ਆਪਹਿ ਉਪਾਇਓ ॥
ਆਪਹਿ ਬਾਪ ਆਪ ਹੀ ਮਾਇਓ ॥ ਆਪਹਿ ਸੂਖਮ ਆਪਹਿ ਅਸਥੂਲਾ ॥

In the beginning, in the middle, and in the end, is Nirankar, the Formless Lord. By Himself is the Sunn and Himself in the peaceful posture; He Himself listens to His Own Praises. He Himself created Himself. HE is Own Father and Own Mother. Himself is subtle and etheric; Himself is manifest and obvious. (Guru Granth Sahib: 250)

The Sunn mentioned above is the State where Ekankar is present in Samadhi. There is nothingness there.

Gurbani hymns state that there in Sunn the profound presence of "*Hukam*". Nothing else can be known as it is misty.

The Hukam is intent and a form of command which creates all the forms and everything else existing in the world. The creation is self-expression of the Ekankar. The Hukam and Shabad heard as celestial sound vibration are the building blocks.

The creation is known as a *Maya Construct*. The Maya is like an illusion. It presents the world where our ignorance of Sach is reinforced. First by limiting the Conscious Awareness and attaching the *Haume* with it. This Haume is our sense of individuality. It creates our personality and as part of our Subtle Body takes repeated births.

The word "ongkaar" represents the Hukam and the Shabad creating form. The *ong-* means Sound and *kaar* -means form. The formless thus creates the form- an opposite of its own formless nature.

What is seen, perceived and apparent to us about creation is Duality known as *Sargun*. All creation is Sargun in nature as it has attributes and qualities. The Sach, however, is present as Nirgun, meaning without qualities and attributes. The *Nirgun* has no form.

Indications of Nirgun show an indirect presence in our world. These are the keys to connect with Nirgun. The keys then bring blessing of the Nirgun as Nadar(vision) which lets us have Conscious awareness to know and perceive the Sach. These aspects of *Sach* are known as *Naam*. The word *Satnaam* in the Mool Mantar explains this part of reality.

The Jap Meditation has Naam in its core for acceptance by the mind. In Creation only the essence of the True One is Naam. The truth is purity. Its quality is to remain immaculate. The truth is steady, and everlasting. Thus the Guru calls the hidden essence as "Satt" (the true) so that we can identify with it.

The Shabad can be heard within us at the Nirgun Point known as Charnarbind in Gurbani. And the Hukam is perceived in the perfectness of Creation despite the complexity.

The beings in creation have the spark of life, a conscious awareness. The body of beings has form. This body has senses and an elaborate biosystem that lets the mind within the brain think and function. In the creation is also the ever movement of the ticking time. There is linear past, the present and the future in our world. This is because our world is ever changing.

So engrossed are we in our transcient petty affairs that there before us is a clossal failure. We fail to see the nature of conscious awareness hidden behind our Haume.

We think ourselves as having power in this world. The haume has built us a false egoistic world. Reality is that we are under Karmic law which is simplicity in itself. What we sow by means of thought and action bringus the events on our life forming the life we live.

The Guru tells that the Ekankar is present in creation as *Karta Purakh.*

The Purakh means infinite all-pervading presence. In every part, visible or invisible is the presence of Purakh.

The entire expanse of the universe has living vibrating presence of Purakh - the light that shines bringing creation an alive flowing force. This presence is actual karta, the doer.

The Hukam is presence of Karta. Our conscious awareness is the same light that is of the Purakh. We are like the waves on water.

A simple meditation to focus on Karta is to think who is talking, who moves the hands, who walks and who perceives the thinking. Who is the observor. We then would have an inkling that the observor is our true nature.

In Gurbani are three aspects of the *Purakh* . The *Karta Purakh,* actual doer; the *Akal Purakh*, the timeless eternal nature of the Purakh and *Satguru Purakh*, the Guru Guide who talks with us, guides us in our Spiritual endeavour. The Gurbani words are known as Shabad Guru. These words are the Satguru's Guru guide in word form.

The next word in the Mool Mantar is Nirbhau. The word "*Nir*" means no, while "*bhau*" means fear. The Mool Mantar here specifically reveals that the fear is not part of the Ekankar. Fear thus is part of duality and is a created emotion. The Nirgun thus has no fear. This is the reason for feeling of peace during even simple meditations.

The Sach is also *"Nirvair"*. This word means "no enmity". In our world forgiveness, benevolence, , peace, freedom and similar feelings characterize the truth. These qualities are a variation of love. When we do not express resentment or resistance then we are nearer to Sach. In fact Love feeling toward the Karta or Satguru lets us identify with truth.

The Guru explains an quality of Sach in "Akal Moorat". Akal is eternal, ever existing sameness. The Moorat is an image or appearance.

The Sach is not within life-death cycle and neither directly experiences past as memory and future as anxiety. The Guru thus tells us that we are living in time where as our perception of the Creator should be that which does not experiences time.

The *Akal Moorat* does not take birth so has no death. The Mool is Ajooni, indicating a formless character. The forms in creation are classified in groups and species. The formless Mool (the Origin of all) is *Ajooni* meaning is not like a species where similar ones exist. Ekankar is one and only one. So Ekarkar self-exists and Self-creates. This aspect is called *Saibhang* in the Mool Mantar.

For our part, we have to learn to know Sach, the Creator as formless. The Karta is our Conscious awareness in purity while Haume the living personality. The Love is a feeling we can experience in the core of our heart. These are Sach and the Naam. The path towards Nirgun is within us. To perceive the *Sach* we have to go within where there is the inner voice of *Satguru*, the True Guru guide.

The opening up of our conscious awareness is the *Nadar* the satguru bestows on us. This is the meaning of "*Gur Prashad*" in the Mool Mantar.

This also means, that the understanding of the Mool Mantar is bestowed by the Guru on the loving devotee.

Gurbani explains in these quotes from the Gurbani hymns:

ਕਹੁ ਨਾਨਕ ਹਰਿ ਆਪਿ ਮਿਲਾਏ ਮਿਲਿ ਸਤਿਗੁਰ ਪੁਰਖ ਸੁਖੁ ਹੋਈ ॥
Says Nanak, the Har (Lord) Himself causes us to meet; on meeting Satguru Purakh, the peace is obtained, (Guru Granth Sahib: 572).

ਸਤਿਗੁਰੁ ਮਿਲਿਆ ਤਾ ਹਰਿ ਪਾਇਆ ਬਿਨੁ ਹਰਿ ਨਾਵੈ ਮੁਕਤਿ ਨ ਹੋਈ ॥
When Satguru (True Guru) is met then is found Har (the infinite God); without the Har Naam (the truth perception), there is no liberation. (Guru Granth Sahib: 770).

These Gurbani words make clear an important point. That there is no intermediatary living person who is the Guru. The Gurbani explicitly states that Satguru meaning the True Guru is *Purakh*.

The Guru has abilities and reach beyond any living person.
For ages, people have been searching for God and only those who accepted within the presence of the Satguru could know God. The Guru says:

ਗੁਰ ਪਰਸਾਦੀ ਸਚੁ ਸਚੇ ਸਚੁ ਲਹਿਆ ॥
By Gur Prashad, is received the truth and the truest of the True. (Guru Granth Sahib :961).

Jap

In the last part of the Mool Mantar, the method "to know and be" true is stated. The word Jap is a meditation technique. Jap is the way to go and stay connected within.
Jap is done by reading, musical rendering, listening and thinking of Sach.

The nature of Sach is told in the last lines of the Mool Mantar

Gurmeet Singh

after Jap indicating the hidden aspects of the technique.

The illustration below explains the hidden message:

Aadh *(Before beginning)*	*Jugad* (After beginning)	Hai Bhee (The present Now)	Hosee Bhee (The future)
Sach	*Sach*	*Sach*	*Sach*

The top line indicates linear time. The second line shows the unchanging nature of Sach. It also shows the presence of Sach prior to creation and after the end of creation. Sach is eternal, beyond time but has given rise to time. It also indicates that anything other than Sach which is created part, is not eternal.

These lines indicate the technique for Jap. This has been explained in the Chapter on Jap at the end.

After the Mool Mantar, the Guru then begins the elaboration. This baani is the Jap Meditation of thought. It means that the meaning is not restricted to the lines but are pointers for doing contemplation of relevant personal or social life.
The baani has hidden within the lines the knowledge that has immense significance. This is revealed when we are in meditative state known as *"Unmann"*. This is explained again in the chapter on Jap Meditation.

Next comes *Pauris* which literally mean a ladder, step, or stair, it is a form of stanza. The Jap Meditation with knowledge and awakening happens as we go along step wise.

At the cost of repetition, it is emphasized again that **the first key** is to go within.

Keep conscious awareness inside even while eyes are open. The initial Jap is to repeat the Mool Manter while listening to your own quietly voiced words. The Gurumanter prevalent from Guru's time is "Waheguru". It is call to the Guru within. It also represents the Creator. This also expresses wonder at the enormous creation. This Gurumanter is to be used for Jap whenever felt.

Second key is "feeling".

The Creator has no form, color, creed but can only be felt with a loving feeling. Creator God is perceived only in awareness.

These two keys' take you within where the significance of the simple appearing words of Japji Pauris come up with deep meanings.

Jap Meditation Steps - Pauris

Pauri means step. The translation of 38 pauries are followed by comments indicating the direction for contemplation. The words have deep meaning giving direction. Gurbani is always to be read in a contemplative mood and slowly. Go within to understand the meaning. There is always inner guidance. Go within to hear and talk with Satguru. Believe and it would appear is the way of Jap meditation.

Jap Meditation Flow through Nadar, which opens the Conscious awareness (Surt}

Dharam Khand: (Karma Experience, Birth Cycles)
Good Karma brings Nadar
Gyan Khand: (Meets Guru Guide; insightful knowledge)
Jap meditation to meet the Satguru Presence
Shram Khand: (Gives up Mera-Tera (Mine-Yours), attachments)
Jap Meditation to die to Haume by identifying with Karta.
Hears Anhad Shabad at Nirgun Point
Karam Khand
(Feels Hazuri (presence), Has control over five passions)
Jap Meditation on Charan Kamal for opening of Tenth Door.
Sach Khand

Gurmeet Singh

(Opening of tenth Door; Illuminated within, Anand)
Jap meditation for Sehej; Jyote of Karta instead of Haume

4. Pauris from 1 to 38

(The Pauris - Steps)

Pauri 1 Defines Purity.
Pauri 2 Explains Hukam.
Pauri 3 Identifying with truth explained.
Pauri 4 What way to adopt.
Pauri 5 Gurmukh.
Pauri 6 Good Karmic Actions.
Pauri 7 Real Greatness.
Pauri 8 Listening takes you within.
Pauri 9 Listening keeps us within.
Pauri 10 Listening brings Peace.
Pauri 11 Listening-Unreachable is felt present.
Pauri 12 Mind Acceptance.
Pauri 13 Mind accepts and aligns with Truth.
Pauri 14 Acceptance builds Dharmic Virtues.
Pauri 15 Acceptance of Truth brings liberation.
Pauri 16 Controlling five passions.
Pauri 17 Countless ways.
Pauri 18 Countless ways but remain firm.
Pauri 19 The role of Thoughts.
Pauri 20 Only Naam can wash impurity of sins.
Pauri 21 True Pilgrimage.
Pauri 22 Infinite Creation.
Pauri 23 True Greatness.
Pauri 24 How much Exalted is the Creator.
Pauri 25 The True Devotional method.
Pauri 26 Priceless is steadfast Devotional Service.
Pauri 27 The dwelling place of Creator God.

Pauri 28 To win the mind is to win the world.
Pauri 29 The Naad vibrates in all.
Pauri 30 Maya's deception created by three forces.
Pauri 31 All Creation is created once for all.
Pauri 32 From Duality, Two to One.
Pauri 33 The Self has no own power.
Pauri 34 The Earth is school of Dharm.
Pauri 35 Opening up to Knowledge of Truth.
Pauri 36 Into the formless world.
Pauri 37 Oneness with Truth, Sach khand.
Pauri 38 Nadar, the vision that opens awareness.

Pauri 1

ਸੋਚੈ ਸੋਚਿ ਨ ਹੋਵਈ ਜੇ ਸੋਚੀ ਲਖ ਵਾਰ ॥
Sochai Soch N Hovee Jae Sochee Lakh Vaar.
By washing, purity (in mind) cannot be achieved, even if we bath a million times.

ਚੁਪੈ ਚੁਪ ਨ ਹੋਵਈ ਜੇ ਲਾਇ ਰਹਾ ਲਿਵ ਤਾਰ ॥
Chupai Chup N Hovee Jae Laae Rehaa Liv Taar.
By remaining silent, inner quiteness is not obtained, even by keeping attentive focus within.

ਭੁਖਿਆ ਭੁਖ ਨ ਉਤਰੀ ਜੇ ਬੰਨਾ ਪੁਰੀਆ ਭਾਰ ॥
Bhukhia Bhukh N utharee Jae Bannaa Pureeaa Bhaar.
By fasting the hunger (desires) are not appeased, even with piled up loads of worldly goods.

ਸਹਸ ਸਿਆਣਪਾ ਲਖ ਹੋਹਿ ਤ ਇਕ ਨ ਚਲੈ ਨਾਲਿ ॥
Sehas Siaanapaa Lakh Hohi Th Eik N Chalai Naal.
One may be adept in hundreds of thousands of smart ways, but not even one of them goes along in the end (making one awakened).

ਕਿਵ ਸਚਿਆਰਾ ਹੋਈਐ ਕਿਵ ਕੂੜੈ ਤੁਟੈ ਪਾਲਿ ॥
Kiv Sachiaaraa Hoeeai Kiv Koorrai Tuttai Paal.
So how can one attain purity? And how can the bonds of falseness be broken?

ਹੁਕਮਿ ਰਜਾਈ ਚਲਣਾ ਨਾਨਕ ਲਿਖਿਆ ਨਾਲਿ ॥੧॥
Hukam Rajaaee Chalanaa Nanak Likhiaa Naal||1|| Says Nanak, move ahead living attuned to the Hukam.

Comments:

This pauri defines purity. We have bonds of attachments and the five vices. These are attached to Haume, our self identity. These bonds are removed when we understand the nature of Haume by understanding the Hukam. Hukam Razai is living without resistance and Oneness.

Pauri 2

ਹੁਕਮੀ ਹੋਵਨਿ ਆਕਾਰ ਹੁਕਮੁ ਨ ਕਹਿਆ ਜਾਈ ॥
Hukamee Hovan Aakaar Hukam N Kehiaa Jaaee.
As is the Hukam, so are created the forms; the manner of Hukam's functioning cannot be described.

ਹੁਕਮੀ ਹੋਵਨਿ ਜੀਅ ਹੁਕਮਿ ਮਿਲੈ ਵਡਿਆਈ ॥
Hukamee Hovan Jeea Hukam Milai Vaddiaaee.
As per Hukam, the beings take life; by the Hukam they achieve (spiritual aim) and get appreciated.

ਹੁਕਮੀ ਉਤਮੁ ਨੀਚੁ ਹੁਕਮਿ ਲਿਖਿ ਦੁਖ ਸੁਖ ਪਾਈਅਹਿ ॥
Hukamee Uttam Neech Hukam Likh Dhukh Sukh Paaeeahi.
As per Hukam, some are high and some are low; the pain and pleasure too are obtained in accord with the system of the Hukam.

ਇਕਨਾ ਹੁਕਮੀ ਬਖਸੀਸ ਇਕਿ ਹੁਕਮੀ ਸਦਾ ਭਵਾਈਅਹਿ ॥
Eikanaa Hukmee Baksees Eik Hukmee Sadhaa Bhavaaeeahi.
Some, in the Hukam, get blessed; and some others, as per system of Hukam, get to wander away always.

ਹੁਕਮੈ ਅੰਦਰਿ ਸਭੁ ਕੋ ਬਾਹਰਿ ਹੁਕਮ ਨ ਕੋਇ ॥
Hukamai Andhar Sabh Ko Baahar Hukam N Koe. Everyone and everything is within the Hukam; nothing is outside the Hukam.

ਨਾਨਕ ਹੁਕਮੈ ਜੇ ਬੁਝੈ ਤ ਹਉਮੈ ਕਹੈ ਨ ਕੋਇ ॥੨॥
Nanak Hukamai Jae Bujhai Taa Houmai Kehai N Koe.
Says Nanak, one who gets to understand the Hukam, does not then speak in Haume.

Comments:

Haume refers to the perception and thinking in terms of our

individual identity. It makes for our self-identity.

Hukam is divine expression like a command or a will that created creation with perfectness to make it function. Hukam spans the whole sphere of the world whether physical, social, the thoughts, the cycles, the karma, both the visible and the invisible. We are part of Hukam in everything - the body, the mind, the thoughts and consciousness.

The Haume is reflected in our attitude, beliefs, behaviour and thinking. It is also reflected in the relationships be built with objects, persons, our abilities, our achievements, our work. These are all attributed to self and forms part of our attachment.

The Gurbani lines however states that when we would understand the Hukam then we would not be having Haume. Such a state would come as we begin to understand and know about Hukam.

An example to understand Hukam is a computer. The hardware is the visible form whereas within it is a Programme with scripts. The Programme is known only to the maker. The Hukam in this world makes possible the creation and its functioning.

This search involves knowing about the nature of reality and above all the self.

We are souls, but what constitutes the soul. How souls have a conscious awareness. Is Soul a single unit or is composed? The Gurbani above is hinting about secrets of conscious awareness. Through Gurbani we come come to know that this awareness is part of Purakh. We are part of whole.

Pauri 3

(The word Gaavai means singing, reading, contemplating)

ਗਾਵੈ ਕੋ ਤਾਣੁ ਹੋਵੈ ਕਿਸੈ ਤਾਣੁ ॥
Gaavai Ko Taan Hovai Kisai Taan.
People Sing about HIS absolute Power – and that none else has that power.

ਗਾਵੈ ਕੋ ਦਾਤਿ ਜਾਣੈ ਨੀਸਾਣੁ ॥
Gaavai Ko Dhaat Jaanai Nisaan.
Those who sing are given gift of knowing about the ways to know HIM.

ਗਾਵੈ ਕੋ ਗੁਣ ਵਡਿਆਈਆ ਚਾਰ ॥
Gaavai Ko Gun Vaddiaaeeaa Chaar.
So sing about the vast glorious virtues of the God.

ਗਾਵੈ ਕੋ ਵਿਦਿਆ ਵਿਖਮੁ ਵੀਚਾਰੁ ॥
Gaavai Ko Vidhiaa Vikham Veechaar.
The singing equals knowledge garnered through the difficult studies.

ਗਾਵੈ ਕੋ ਸਾਜਿ ਕਰੇ ਤਨੁ ਖੇਹ ॥
Gaavai Ko Saaj Karae Than Khaeh.
Sing about how the body (person) who is just a dust gets fashioned.

ਗਾਵੈ ਕੋ ਜੀਅ ਲੈ ਫਿਰਿ ਦੇਹ ॥
Gaavai Ko Jeea Lai Fir Dhaeh.
Sing about HIS power to take life and even give back.

ਗਾਵੈ ਕੋ ਜਾਪੈ ਦਿਸੈ ਦੂਰਿ ॥
Gaavai Ko Japai Dhisai Dhoor.
Sing so that the HE appearing far is then seen near.

ਗਾਵੈ ਕੋ ਵੇਖੈ ਹਾਦਰਾ ਹਦੂਰਿ ॥
Gaavai Ko Vaekhai Haadharaa Hadhoor.

Sing so thay HIS presence is seen so near.

ਕਥਨਾ ਕਥੀ ਨ ਆਵੈ ਤੋਟਿ ॥
Kathhanaa Kathhee N Aavai Thott.
Even by keep saying there is never shortage of something to sing about.

ਕਥਿ ਕਥਿ ਕਥੀ ਕੋਟੀ ਕੋਟਿ ਕੋਟਿ ॥
Kathh Kathh Kathhee Kottee Kott Kott.
Millions upon millions speak about HIM.

ਦੇਦਾ ਦੇ ਲੈਦੇ ਥਕਿ ਪਾਹਿ ॥
Dhaedhaa Dhae Laidhae Thhak Paahi.
The Great Giver keeps fulfilling, while those who live grow weary.

ਜੁਗਾ ਜੁਗੰਤਰਿ ਖਾਹੀ ਖਾਹਿ ॥
Jugaa Juganthar Khaahee Khaahi.
Throughout the ages,
the receivers (living beings) keep using the worldly boons (resources).

ਹੁਕਮੀ ਹੁਕਮੁ ਚਲਾਏ ਰਾਹੁ ॥
Hukamee Hukam Chalaaeae Raahu.
Owner of Hukam, built with Hukam the life path.
ਨਾਨਕ ਵਿਗਸੈ ਵੇਪਰਵਾਹੁ ॥੩॥
Nanak Vigasai Vaeparavaahu.
Says Nanak, HE HIMSELF is ever in bloom and unruffled. ॥3॥

Comments:

This pauri comes in sequence after about the *Sachiar* (pure), Hukam Razai, Hukam and Haume. Here the Gurbani is explaining the worldly life secrets and building up of relationship.

This is how Jap is done in daily life. All of Gurbani is JAP that brings a relationship with the formless and unseen known through the underlying workings of the Hukam. Living in Haume we are ignorant about Hukam. It is when we sing the right kind of praises that the nearness develops. The praises are names that speak of the qualities. We speak, become respectful, loving and all along identify.

The Gurbani Kirtan (singing of hymns) may look like praises - a kind of appeasement. The Gurbani however makes clear that that The ONE being praised is unaffected and unruffled. **The Creator needs nothing.**

This singing is a way to develop loving relationship. it is a way to identify with truth. This also is the way to bring to fore the hidden working of Hukam. The true one is formless. The Jap with feeling along with seeing the nearness, brings the *Hazuri* (awareness of presence).

This pauri gives with another significant indication. Are we building our life path our self or walking the path Hukam has laid down for us? Is there destiny. The answer is contextual- both yes and no.

Even when in Haume then we are functioning in Hukam. And when within in awareness of *Sach* (truth) then there is only one "player". The Haume too is a play like the worldly life which is like a dream. It looks real when we are living the life but is transcient.

Pauri 4

ਸਾਚਾ ਸਾਹਿਬੁ ਸਾਚੁ ਨਾਇ ਭਾਖਿਆ ਭਾਉ ਅਪਾਰੁ ॥
Sacha Sahib Sach Naae Bhaakhiaa Bhaao Apaar.
The true part is that of the Master, this truth is Naam; HIS speech is infinite love.

ਆਖਹਿ ਮੰਗਹਿ ਦੇਹਿ ਦੇਹਿ ਦਾਤਿ ਕਰੇ ਦਾਤਾਰੁ ॥
Aakhehi Mangehi Dhaehi Dhaehi Dhaath Karae Dataar.
We ask, we pray for boons from the *Dataar* (the God).

ਫੇਰਿ ਕਿ ਅਗੈ ਰਖੀਐ ਜਿਤੁ ਦਿਸੈ ਦਰਬਾਰੁ ॥
Faer K Agai Rakheeai Jith Dhisai Dharabaar.
So what offering do we have to give, so that we might see HIS Court.

ਮੁਹੌ ਕਿ ਬੋਲਣੁ ਬੋਲੀਐ ਜਿਤੁ ਸੁਣਿ ਧਰੇ ਪਿਆਰੁ ॥
Muha K Bolan Boleeai Jith Sun Dhharae Piaar.
What words should we speak, which make us feel love for HIM.

ਅੰਮ੍ਰਿਤ ਵੇਲਾ ਸਚੁ ਨਾਉ ਵਡਿਆਈ ਵੀਚਾਰੁ ॥
Amrit Velaa Sach Naao Vadiaae Veechaar.
The *Amrit Velaa* (the ambrosial hours before dawn), is the time for Sach Naam, with *vadiaae (singing praises through Shabad kirtan)* or contemplation.

ਕਰਮੀ ਆਵੈ ਕਪੜਾ ਨਦਰੀ ਮੋਖੁ ਦੁਆਰੁ ॥
Karamee Aavai Kaparraa Nadaree Mokh Duar.
By karmic actions we are dressed up to obtain the *Nadar*, which shows us the gate of Liberation.

ਨਾਨਕ ਏਵੈ ਜਾਣੀਐ ਸਭੁ ਆਪੇ ਸਚਿਆਰੁ ॥੪॥
Nanak Eaevai Jaaneeai Sabh Aapae Sachiaar.
Says Nanak, know in this way, we come to know that all (everything) is the true ONE. ||4||

Comments:

The use of the word Sach has a significance. The feature of truth is permanence and a reality which all the time remains same. In contrast the created aspect does not have this characteristic. Anything transitory, subject to life-death is not "true".

This idea is central to identify Naam, which is the Sach. The Jap of Gurbani is to know and identify with the truth. This awareness comes when "Nadar" is received.

> The word Nadar has Arabic/Punjabi origin and means" vision". The Nadar brings awareness and understanding. Nadar can be understood as Divine blessing of Satguru.

The Ambrosial hour is the time when influence of Maya is less. This is time for Jap either through attentive reading, active singing, Jap or contemplation within.

Naam is the name for Sach (truth). As the word suggests, to take a name is to know. And to know this is same as one ownself then the taking of name is to identify.
The Naam is understood through the Guru. Gurbani talks of *Sach* its hymns were uttered through those who were one with truth. These were the Saints and the Guru's that had Guru Jyote (light) transferred by the First Guru "Guru Nanak".

The origin of these Hymns is the Shabad, heard as the sound like vibration of creation. The thoughts in our mind are part of created Sargun. The Originating Shabad is heard within our head when Nadar (perceptive vision) comes. Attention is kept there by hearing in Jap Meditation.

Pauri 5

ਥਾਪਿਆ ਨ ਜਾਇ ਕੀਤਾ ਨ ਹੋਇ ॥
Thhaapiaa N Jaae Keethaa N Hoe.
The Sach can neither be placed nor come there by doing something.

ਆਪੇ ਆਪਿ ਨਿਰੰਜਨੁ ਸੋਇ ॥
Aapae Aap Niranjan Soe.
The Sach exists by itself and is HIS immaculate Self.

ਜਿਨਿ ਸੇਵਿਆ ਤਿਨਿ ਪਾਇਆ ਮਾਨੁ ॥
Jin Saeviaa Thin Paaeiaa Maan.
Those who serve (through Jap) are honored.

ਨਾਨਕ ਗਾਵੀਐ ਗੁਣੀ ਨਿਧਾਨੁ ॥
Nanak Gaaveeai Gunee Nidhhaan.
Says Nanak, sing of HIS qualities, the real treasure.

ਗਾਵੀਐ ਸੁਣੀਐ ਮਨਿ ਰਖੀਐ ਭਾਉ ॥
Gaaveeai Suneeai Man Rakheeai Bhaao.
During singing, and listening, let your mind be filled with love.

ਦੁਖੁ ਪਰਹਰਿ ਸੁਖੁ ਘਰਿ ਲੈ ਜਾਇ ॥
Dhukh Parehar Sukh Ghar Lai Jaae.
The pain shall go away, and peace is brought in the self-home.

ਗੁਰਮੁਖਿ ਨਾਦੰ ਗੁਰਮੁਖਿ ਵੇਦੰ ਗੁਰਮੁਖਿ ਰਹਿਆ ਸਮਾਈ ॥
Gurmukh Naadan Gurmukh Vaedhan Gurmukh Rehiaa Samaee.
Gurmukh hears the Naad (Anhad Shabad); Gurmukh receives understanding; Gurmukh comes to know that HIS presence is everywhere and in everything.
(Word Vedan comes from Veda which means understanding, here reference is not of Vedic literature)

ਗੁਰੁ ਈਸਰੁ ਗੁਰੁ ਗੋਰਖੁ ਬਰਮਾ ਗੁਰੁ ਪਾਰਬਤੀ ਮਾਈ ॥

Gur Isher Gur Gorakh Baramaa Gur Paarabathee Maaee. (For the Gurmukh) The Guru is within (the word *Isher* means 'inside") the Guru is Gorakh - meaning spiritual head; the Guru is *Parvati* (meaning divine strength and power).
(The *Parvati* is wife of Shiva, the force of destruction);

ਜੇ ਹਉ ਜਾਣਾ ਆਖਾ ਨਾਹੀ ਕਹਣਾ ਕਥਨੁ ਨ ਜਾਈ ॥

Jae Ho Jaanaa Aakhaa Naahee Kehanaa Kathhan N Jaaee. Even on knowing Sach, one cannot express nor can described in words.

ਗੁਰਾ ਇਕ ਦੇਹਿ ਬੁਝਾਈ ॥
ਸਭਨਾ ਜੀਆ ਕਾ ਇਕੁ ਦਾਤਾ ਸੋ ਮੈ ਵਿਸਰਿ ਨ ਜਾਈ ॥੫॥

Guraa Eik Dhaehi Bujhaaee. Sabhanaa Jeeaa Kaa Eik Datta Soo Maei Visar N Jaaee ||5||
Guru has made me understand that one should never forget that there is only ONE giver for all beings. ||5||

Comments:

The *Sacha Sahib* does not come to get established, in an idol or photo or person or anything.
HE exists in purity, independent and unaffected.
No mantra can affect or bind the *Sach*. This is an indication that we should not fall prey to any such claim. Sach is not under anyone's control or does their bidding.

The Guru next tells us that we should serve the Master. The spiritual terminology is invariably indirect. So, by serving is meant to be humble and sing the virtues so as to develop love.

Understanding come when there is the attitude of a "Gurmukh". This involves accepting the words of the Guru as truth. The *Sach* is **very** subtle. Obedience and acceptance, comes first and the experience comes next.

The Gurmukh hear the Naad, which is Anhad Shabad. This means the Gurmukh with Jap has gone deep within. The Gurmukh then hears this Naad within.

The understanding to go within is granted by the Guru. This happens within but greatest understanding the Guru gives is awareness of HIS presence outside and within. The True Guru is met within. The Gurbani names the Guru within as *Satguru*, commonly translation is "True Guru".

On looking at the word "*Satt*", the message that comes is *Satguru* is *Sacha* (True ONE) Ownself. Gurbani is also Satt. The Shabad within is Satt. And so also the conscious awareness without Haume is Satt.

The other parts of the line *Gur Isher,* where the word *Isher* means "one who is within "confirms that no living person can be Satguru as no human has this ability to be with all all the time. The *Satguru* Gurbani says is also Purakh. The Guru by use of some specific words is giving hints for shift in thinking.

By the word "*Datta*" the Guru is giving the message that all that is there in this world is HIS creation and HIS gift to use. These do not truly belong to us.

Our body, house, car, business, wealth, food, clothes and even success or career all are given by him. It is our Haume which considers there our own. The Haume this way brings about attachment. We thereby suffer whenever there is loss. With no attachment the suffering simply fades away.

This attachment is because of presence of Maya in the Physical world. When we shift *Surt* (conscious awareness) within then the effect of Maya is gone. The way revealed by Guru Nanak is to keep awareness within by hearing the *Anhad Shabad.*

Pauri 6

ਤੀਰਥਿ ਨਾਵਾ ਜੇ ਤਿਸੁ ਭਾਵਾ ਵਿਣੁ ਭਾਣੇ ਕਿ ਨਾਇ ਕਰੀ ॥
Theerathh Naavaa Jae This Bhaavaa Vin Bhaanae K Naae Karee.
The cleansing bath at place of pilgrimage happens when Without pleasing HIM, what good are ritual cleansings?

ਜੇਤੀ ਸਿਰਠਿ ਉਪਾਈ ਵੇਖਾ ਵਿਣੁ ਕਰਮਾ ਕਿ ਮਿਲੈ ਲਈ ॥
Jaethee Sirath Oupaaee Vaekhaa Vin Karamaa K Milai Lae.
Whichever created beings are seen around: without the karma of good actions, can they get to meet?

ਮਤਿ ਵਿਚਿ ਰਤਨ ਜਵਾਹਰ ਮਾਣਿਕ ਜੇ ਇਕ ਗੁਰ ਕੀ ਸਿਖ ਸੁਣੀ ॥
Matt Vich Rattan Javahar Maanik Jae Eik Gur Kee Sikh Sunee.
Within the mind are gems, jewels and rubies, if once the Sikh of the Guru listens.

ਗੁਰਾ ਇਕ ਦੇਹਿ ਬੁਝਾਈ ॥ ਸਭਨਾ ਜੀਆ ਕਾ ਇਕੁ ਦਾਤਾ ਸੋ ਮੈ ਵਿਸਰਿ ਨ ਜਾਈ ॥੬॥
Guraa Eik Dhaehi Bujhaaee. Sabhanaa Jeeaa Kaa Eik Dhaathaa So Mai Visar N Jaaee ||6||
Guru has made me understand that I should never forget that there is only ONE giver for all beings.

Comments:
The Maya has a hold over our way of thinking and attitudes. We are diverted to pursuits trying to obtain something thereby preventing us from taking the right path.

Pilgrimage is one such action. The Guru here is pointing out that within the mind lies the gems ang jewels - meaning precious path.

The emphasis is on not forgetting the Creator who has given us all the objects and life in this world.

We need to understand the above fact as this shifts our attitude. The attitude to be build is to stop our attachment to these. We need not consider these as ours. We think that the life that we are living is our achievement. The intelligence is ours. The success of an effort is "us". We forget that without the Hukam nothing is achieved.

In fact, there is only Hukam in play. The attitude change comes from observation and thought. Observe the perfect working of nature.

An example shows this clearly. A cricketer hits a shot which goes for a six. There is whole nature involved in this. The speed of the ball, right placement of ball on bat and the force. The air flow at the time. The direction of the hit. The nature contrived to perfectly bring conclusion of an intention. There could have been a miss, leading to stumping. Or there could have been less force in the movement, a different angle of the bat, air flow could have been different. Anything could have been different. But the universe contrived to keep the perfect conditions for the outcome.

Same way reflect on how things happened in your life. At all the time the underlying Hukam makes things function perfectly. We may say this is how nature and the physical laws work. But what are these. What lets these exist.

In the present day the science itself has uncovered enough evidence to show the connection of the mind with the matter. There is even sharing of knowing something.

As Gurmukh if we look at the Guru's words and do contemplation the understanding would come.

The aim is to move away from Haume attachment by attributing ownership. This would prevent lot of suffering.

Haume prevents Sach from coming to fore. They do not remain together. So, when within then the thought should be that each body part is run by HIM and that even the consciousness is HIS.

You are not there. The awareness is HIS. This is the state without Haume which is kept asserted as Jap.

Pauri 7

ਜੇ ਜੁਗ ਚਾਰੇ ਆਰਜਾ ਹੋਰ ਦਸੂਣੀ ਹੋਇ ॥
Jae Jugg Chaarae Aarajaa Hor Dhasoonee Hoe.
Even if you could live throughout the four ages, or even ten times more,

ਨਵਾ ਖੰਡਾ ਵਿਚਿ ਜਾਣੀਐ ਨਾਲਿ ਚਲੈ ਸਭੁ ਕੋਇ ॥
Navaa Khandaa Vich Jaaneeai Naal Chalai Sabh Koe.
And even if you were known throughout the nine continents and followed by all,

ਚੰਗਾ ਨਾਉ ਰਖਾਇ ਕੈ ਜਸੁ ਕੀਰਤਿ ਜਗਿ ਲੇਇ ॥
Changaa Naao Rakhaae Kai Jas Keerath Jag Laee.
Having a name and reputation, with praise and fame throughout the world-

ਜੇ ਤਿਸੁ ਨਦਰਿ ਨ ਆਵਈ ਤ ਵਾਤ ਨ ਪੁਛੈ ਕੇ ॥
Jae This Nadhar N Aavee Th Vaath N Pushhai Kae.
Still, if the Lord does not bless you with the Nadar (Gift of awareness), then who cares?

ਕੀਟਾ ਅੰਦਰਿ ਕੀਟੁ ਕਰਿ ਦੋਸੀ ਦੋਸੁ ਧਰੇ ॥
Keettaa Andhar Keett Kar Dhosee Dhos Dhharae.
The condition is that of a lowly worm among worms, and even contemptible among sinners.

ਨਾਨਕ ਨਿਰਗੁਣਿ ਗੁਣੁ ਕਰੇ ਗੁਣਵੰਤਿਆ ਗੁਣੁ ਦੇ ॥
Nanak Nirgun Gunn Karae Gunvanthiaa Gunn Dhae.
Says Nanak, God blesses the unworthy with virtue, and bestows virtue on the virtue seeker.

ਤੇਹਾ ਕੋਇ ਨ ਸੁਝਈ ਜਿ ਤਿਸੁ ਗੁਣੁ ਕੋਇ ਕਰੇ ॥੭॥
Thaehaa Koe Na Sujhee Jeh Tis Gunn Koe Karae.
No one can even imagine anyone like you who can bestow virtue. ||7||

Comments:

There have been great kings and rulers in the human history. They held great power and had hold over vast land and people. It all was of no avail.

Among these rulers were Ravan (king in ancient time) with his gold houses, rulers in Egypt, the Mongols, the Sikandar of Greece. They are dust and no one cares about them.

The virtues and wealth all are bestowed by HIM. Even a person as lowly as an ant gets to rise up when the great giver bestows Nadar. They become same as HIM.

Pauri 8

ਸੁਣਿਐ ਸਿਧ ਪੀਰ ਸੁਰਿ ਨਾਥ ॥
Suniai Sidhh Peer Sur Naath.
Listening-one becomes the Siddha, the peer, the high master.

ਸੁਣਿਐ ਧਰਤਿ ਧਵਲ ਆਕਾਸ ॥
Suniai Dhharath Dhhaval Aakaas.
Listening- one comes to know about the earth, its support and the sky formation.

ਸੁਣਿਐ ਦੀਪ ਲੋਅ ਪਾਤਾਲ ॥
Suniai Dheep Loa Paathaal.
Listening- one comes to know about the oceans, the lands of the world and the nether regions of the underworld.

ਸੁਣਿਐ ਪੋਹਿ ਨ ਸਕੈ ਕਾਲੁ ॥
Suniai Pohi Na Sakai Kaal.
Listening- the Death cannot even touch.

ਨਾਨਕ ਭਗਤਾ ਸਦਾ ਵਿਗਾਸੁ ॥
Nanak Bhagathaa Sadhaa Vigaas.
Says Nanak, the devotees are forever in bliss.

ਸੁਣਿਐ ਦੂਖ ਪਾਪ ਕਾ ਨਾਸੁ ॥੮॥
Suniai Dhookh Paap Kaa Naas ||8||
Listening- the pain and sin are erased. ||8||

Comments:

The word Sunieh – means "to listen". The Guru has given great importance in three Pauris, to listening since it holds the secret to a transformation.

Listening takes us within. This may seem a simple enough action but this move within is important difference. This is coming in *Sharan* (protection and guidance).

In our everyday life we are very much visual. this means future driven. We hardly process the past or the present. The thoughts about the future mostly brings anxiety. This also means most of the time we are thinking and interacting in the worldly life.

The Mool Mantar explained that *Sach* is Nirbhau (fear is not part of it, meaning fear is not Sach). In the line mention was made of linear time with "*Hehbhi Sach*" indicating the present "now".

Listening shifts focus to the "present" and the attention moves within. Now within is the world of "Nirbhau".

Within is Nirgun world which does not have any attributes. There is no form within it nor any other element of worldly life, even the mind. The formless can be felt within. There is just "Awareness".

The listening is a Jap technique. We listen with feeling of love. We listen to the Gurbani. We listen to the Guru Mantra. In listening we are in the present. By listening we develop the ability to keep focus within even when our eyes are open.

This ability keeps us in the present now. The Sach exists in the Now and Sach creates the Past present too.

(More is explained about Nirgun-Sargun and the Jap technique at the end.)

The secret aspect of *suniye* (listening) is the listening to the *Shabad* sound ever flowing within. *This is known as meeting of Surt (conscious awareness) and the Shabad.*

Pauri 9

ਸੁਣਿਐ ਈਸਰੁ ਬਰਮਾ ਇੰਦੁ ॥
Suniai Eesar Baramaa Eindh.
Listening- comes to know about the *Shiva, Brahma* and *Indra* (three forces in nature).

ਸੁਣਿਐ ਮੁਖਿ ਸਾਲਾਹਣ ਮੰਦੁ ॥
Suniai Mukh Saalaahan Mandh
Listening-even the lowly people begin to praise.

ਸੁਣਿਐ ਜੋਗ ਜੁਗਤਿ ਤਨਿ ਭੇਦ ॥
Suniai Jog Jugath Than Bhaedh.
Listening- comes to know the way to meet and the secret of the body (and the soul within).

ਸੁਣਿਐ ਸਾਸਤ ਸਿਮ੍ਰਿਤਿ ਵੇਦ ॥
Suniai Saasath Simrith Vaedh.
Listening- equals knowing of the Shastras, the Smritis and the Vedas.

ਨਾਨਕ ਭਗਤਾ ਸਦਾ ਵਿਗਾਸੁ ॥
Nanak Bhagathaa Sadhaa Vigaas.
Says Nanak, the devotees are forever in bliss.

ਸੁਣਿਐ ਦੂਖ ਪਾਪ ਕਾ ਨਾਸੁ ॥੯॥
Suniai Dhookh Paap Kaa Naas
Listening-the pain and sin are erased. ||9||

Comments:

Listening places our conscious awareness within. Then we keep up the Jap by means of either the Gurumantar along with thoughts of formless presence. Initially it is "as if present", then actual perception comes.

Feel the proximity of Akal Purakh with love. Do not let Haume attachments disturb you.

This is the way to perceive Hazuri (presence) which definitly comes.

Once Sach experience is there like Hazuri it is kept in awareness again and again.

Pauri 10

ਸੁਣਿਐ ਸਤੁ ਸੰਤੋਖੁ ਗਿਆਨੁ ॥
Suniai Satt Santokh Giaan
Listening- builds truth, contentment and spiritual wisdom.

ਸੁਣਿਐ ਅਠਸਠਿ ਕਾ ਇਸਨਾਨੁ ॥
Suniai Athsath Kaa Eshnaan.
Listening- gives result of cleansing bath at the sixty-eight places of pilgrimage.

ਸੁਣਿਐ ਪੜਿ ਪੜਿ ਪਾਵਹਿ ਮਾਨੁ ॥
Suniai Parh Parh Paavehi Maan.
Listening- while reading, reciting, leads to honor.

ਸੁਣਿਐ ਲਾਗੈ ਸਹਜਿ ਧਿਆਨੁ ॥
Suniai Laagai Sehaj Dhhiaan.
Listening- one easily intuitively reaches meditative state.

ਨਾਨਕ ਭਗਤਾ ਸਦਾ ਵਿਗਾਸੁ ॥
Nanak Bhagathaa Sadhaa Vigaas.
Say Nanak, the devotees are forever in bliss.

ਸੁਣਿਐ ਦੂਖ ਪਾਪ ਕਾ ਨਾਸੁ ॥੧੦॥
Suniai Dhookh Paap Kaa Naas.
Say Nanak, the devotees are forever in bliss.
Listening-the pain and sin are erased. ||10||

Comments:
Two transformative changes that occur when we go within and keep up the listening process:
First the feeling of peace and bliss. **The second** the sufferings begins to go along with Haume. **Third,** the Naam becomes our identity

Pauri 11

ਸੁਣਿਐ ਸਰਾ ਗੁਣਾ ਕੇ ਗਾਹ ॥
Suniai Saraa Gunaa Kae Gaah
On listening- becomes the dweller of vast ocean of virtue.

ਸੁਣਿਐ ਸੇਖ ਪੀਰ ਪਾਤਿਸਾਹ ॥
Suniai Saekh Peer Pathshah.
Listening- one equals the Sheikh, Religious Peer and Emperors.

ਸੁਣਿਐ ਅੰਧੇ ਪਾਵਹਿ ਰਾਹੁ ॥
Suniai Andhhae Paavehi Raahu. Listening- even the blind (about spirituality) finds the Path.

ਸੁਣਿਐ ਹਾਥ ਹੋਵੈ ਅਸਗਾਹੁ ॥
Suniai Haathh Hovai Asagaahu.
Listening-the Unreachable comes within grasp.

ਨਾਨਕ ਭਗਤਾ ਸਦਾ ਵਿਗਾਸੁ ॥
Nanak Bhagathaa Sadhaa Vigaas
Says Nanak, the devotees are forever in bliss.

ਸੁਣਿਐ ਦੂਖ ਪਾਪ ਕਾ ਨਾਸੁ ॥੧੧॥
Suniai Dhookh Paap Kaa Naas.
Listening-the pain and sin are erased. ||11||

Comments:

The *suniye* pauris point towards keeping of conscious awareness within to receive wisdom from within.

Listening takes us within. It makes us familiar with the mindscape within. When within, our mind tries to push awareness out. We are told that inside we have to reach depth. In fact, this word is a misnomer. Inside our conscious awareness has to open up and be able to perceive the presence of Purakh.

Inside we come to perceive the presence of *Satguru Purakh, Karta Purakh, Akal Purakh*.

Purakh presence of *Ekankar* is everywhere.

All are same but difference in name is for our purpose. There is within freedom from fear and anxiety. Within Nirgun is Anhad Shabad- the celestial sound vibration of creation. Gurbani reveals much including that the Soul is not a single unit. It is the Karta Purakh and the Haume. There is further Mind-body combination.

The awareness has to move within and the mind has to attach with the Sach. The imperceptible nature of Sach comes in awareness with the Guru guided Jap Meditation on *Naam*.

The Naam, as explained earlier is the *Sach* as stated in the Mool Mantar. This is the aim of Jap Meditation.

Pauri 12

ਮੰਨੇ ਕੀ ਗਤਿ ਕਹੀ ਨ ਜਾਇ ॥
Mannae Kee Gatt Kehee Na Jaae.
The inner state of person that accepts (believe) cannot be described.

ਜੇ ਕੋ ਕਹੈ ਪਿਛੈ ਪਛੁਤਾਇ ॥
Jae Ko Kehai Pishhai Pashhuthaae.
Anyone who describes then regrets that this was futile effort.

ਕਾਗਦਿ ਕਲਮ ਨ ਲਿਖਣਹਾਰੁ ॥
Kaagadh Kalam N Likhanhaar.
No paper, no pen is sufficient so a scribe can;

ਮੰਨੇ ਕਾ ਬਹਿ ਕਰਨਿ ਵੀਚਾਰੁ ॥
Mannae Kaa Behi Karan Vichar.
We cannot sit and contemplate about this state.

ਐਸਾ ਨਾਮੁ ਨਿਰੰਜਨੁ ਹੋਇ ॥
Aisaa Naam Niranjan Hoe.
Such is the Naam that makes one pure (immaculate).

ਜੇ ਕੋ ਮੰਨਿ ਜਾਣੈ ਮਨਿ ਕੋਇ ॥੧੨॥
Jae Ko Mann Jaanai Man Koe.
This happens with the attitude of acceptance in mind and then through mind the knowing comes. ||12||

(Our minds are limited by our perception and intelligence. The higher awareness is accessible within and opens up perception. The mind's intelligence too adapts.)

Comments:

The pauri speak of Mannae which means acceptance. This is the second part of listening making for the technique of Jap.

The listening takes us within and the mind then accepts the Sach through the Guru.

The Gurbani explains that Naam. The door to Gurbani opens up when we are within. Gurbani word meanings are skipped by mind during reading suddenly appear to indicate a reality.

When Gurbani tells Satguru is ever present within us then we must accept this as absolute truth. What is not in perception or a part of experience yet is to be accepted. The mind's doubting nature is also subdued when we are within.

Within is Nirgun- a timeless world. The *moment mind accepts,* **the Nadar** opens up conscious awareness to bring the Sach experience.

Pauri 13

ਮੰਨੈ ਸੁਰਤਿ ਹੋਵੈ ਮਨਿ ਬੁਧਿ ॥
Mannai Surath Hovai Mann Budhh.
The conscious awareness then comes to be what the mind's intelligence has accepted.

ਮੰਨੈ ਸਗਲ ਭਵਣ ਕੀ ਸੁਧਿ ॥
Mannai Sagal Bhavan Kee Sudhh.
The Mannai comes to know about reality of creation.

ਮੰਨੈ ਮੁਹਿ ਚੋਟਾ ਨਾ ਖਾਇ ॥
Mannai Muhi Chottaa Naa Khaae.
The Mannai does not suffer (due to karmic actions).

ਮੰਨੈ ਜਮ ਕੈ ਸਾਥਿ ਨ ਜਾਇ ॥
Mannai Jam Kai Saathh N Jaae.
The Mannai do not have to go with the Messenger of Death (mythical fear of Death.)

ਐਸਾ ਨਾਮੁ ਨਿਰੰਜਨੁ ਹੋਇ ॥
Aisaa Naam Niranjan Hoe.
Such is the Naam through which one becomes pure.

ਜੇ ਕੋ ਮੰਨਿ ਜਾਣੈ ਮਨਿ ਕੋਇ ॥੧੩॥
Jae Ko Mann Jaanai Man Koe.
This happens with the attitude of acceptance in mind and then through mind the knowing comes. ||13||

Pauri 14

ਮੰਨੈ ਮਾਰਗਿ ਠਾਕ ਨ ਪਾਇ ॥
Mannai Maarag Thaak N Paae.
The path of the Mannai shall never be blocked.

ਮੰਨੈ ਪਤਿ ਸਿਉ ਪਰਗਟੁ ਜਾਇ ॥
Mannai Path Sio Paragatt Jaae.
The Mannai shall depart with honor and fame.

ਮੰਨੈ ਮਗੁ ਨ ਚਲੈ ਪੰਥੁ ॥
Mannai Mag N Chalai Panthh.
The Mannai do not follow empty religious rituals.

ਮੰਨੈ ਧਰਮ ਸੇਤੀ ਸਨਬੰਧੁ ॥
Mannai Dharam Saethee Sanabandhh.
The Mannai are firmly bound to the Dharma.

ਐਸਾ ਨਾਮੁ ਨਿਰੰਜਨੁ ਹੋਇ ॥ ਜੇ ਕੋ ਮੰਨਿ ਜਾਣੈ ਮਨਿ ਕੋਇ ॥੧੪॥
Aisaa Naam Niranjan Hoe. Jae Ko Mann Jaanai Man Koe. Such is the Naam through which one becomes pure . This only one who has this attitude of acceptance can comes to know within. ||14||

Comments:

The Mannai here is an acceptance which also has commitment towards the chosen path. The doubt that comes of others doing attractive rituals and making claims is not allowed to sway the mind.

Pauri 15

ਮੰਨੈ ਪਾਵਹਿ ਮੋਖੁ ਦੁਆਰੁ ॥
Mannai Paavehi Mokh Dhuaar.
The Mannai find the Door of Liberation.

ਮੰਨੈ ਪਰਵਾਰੈ ਸਾਧਾਰੁ ॥
Mannai Paravaarai Saadhhaar.
The family and relations of Mannai to get uplifted.

ਮੰਨੈ ਤਰੈ ਤਾਰੇ ਗੁਰੁ ਸਿਖ ॥
Mannai Tharai Thaarae Gursikh.
The Mannai makes other Gursikhs travel the path.

ਮੰਨੈ ਨਾਨਕ ਭਵਹਿ ਨ ਭਿਖ ॥
Mannai Nanak Bhavehi N Bhikh.
The Mannai, says Nanak, does not wander nor begs.

ਐਸਾ ਨਾਮੁ ਨਿਰੰਜਨੁ ਹੋਇ ॥
Aisaa Naam Niranjan Hoe.
Such is the Naam through which one becomes pure.

ਜੇ ਕੋ ਮੰਨਿ ਜਾਣੈ ਮਨਿ ਕੋਇ ॥੧੫॥
Jae Ko Mann Jaanai Man Koe.
This only one who has this attitude of acceptance can comes to know within. ||15||

Comments:

The importance and the transformation that the attitude of *Mannai* brings has been amply illustrated by the Guru.

Each line has a message and indication for the Jap meditation.

When within the Satguru Guides. The voice is clearly heard. The dialogue can be had with the Purakh.

The next Pauris look at making the vessel of the mind-body suitable so that the Sach then can reside in it.

The next thing the person going within has to contend with are "five passions" also known as thieves. These five are "Lust, Anger, Greed, Attachment and Ego".

In Gurbani the ਪੰਚ Panch also refer to five elements and also the Panch Shabad. Care- the word Panch does not mean chosen one at any place.

Pauri 16

ਪੰਚ ਪਰਵਾਣ ਪੰਚ ਪਰਧਾਨੁ ॥
Panch Paravaan Panch Paradhhaan.
The controller of the five (passions) is accepted.

ਪੰਚੇ ਪਾਵਹਿ ਦਰਗਹਿ ਮਾਨੁ ॥
Panchae Paavehi Dharagehi Maan.
On controlling these five, you would get place of honor in the Court of Sach.

ਪੰਚੇ ਸੋਹਹਿ ਦਰਿ ਰਾਜਾਨੁ ॥
Panchae Sohehi Dhar Raajaan.
The one having the five controlled is adorned like a king on the path.

ਪੰਚਾ ਕਾ ਗੁਰੁ ਏਕੁ ਧਿਆਨੁ ॥
Panchaa Kaa Gur Eaek Dhhiaan.
The way to control the five is to turn the mind within with the Ekankar in mind.

ਜੇ ਕੋ ਕਹੈ ਕਰੈ ਵੀਚਾਰੁ ॥
Jae Ko Kehai Karai Veechaar.
Let one think and contemplate.

ਕਰਤੇ ਕੈ ਕਰਣੈ ਨਾਹੀ ਸੁਮਾਰੁ ॥
Karteh Kai Karanai Naahee Sumaar.
The ways of Creators working are not found.

ਧੌਲੁ ਧਰਮੁ ਦਇਆ ਕਾ ਪੂਤੁ ॥
Dhhaal Dhharam Dhaeiaa Kaa Pooth.
The mythical bull (*thought to be holding the earth on head*) is not the support. Actual support is of Dharma, which is born out of compassion;

ਸੰਤੋਖੁ ਥਾਪਿ ਰਖਿਆ ਜਿਨਿ ਸੂਤਿ ॥

Santhokh Thhaap Rakhiaa Jin Sooth.
The contentment is what holds these together.

ਜੇ ਕੋ ਬੁਝੈ ਹੋਵੈ ਸਚਿਆਰੁ ॥
Jae Ko Bujhai Hovai Sachiaar.
One who discerns this becomes pure.

ਧਵਲੈ ਉਪਰਿ ਕੇਤਾ ਭਾਰੁ ॥
Dhhavalai Oupar Kaethaa Bhaar.
What a great load there is on this bull.

ਧਰਤੀ ਹੋਰੁ ਪਰੈ ਹੋਰੁ ਹੋਰੁ ॥
Dhharathee Hor Parai Hor Hor.
There are so many worlds beyond this world and even many beyond.

ਤਿਸ ਤੇ ਭਾਰੁ ਤਲੈ ਕਵਣੁ ਜੋਰੁ ॥
This Thae Bhaar Thalai Kavan Jor.
What power holds them, and supports their weight.

ਜੀਅ ਜਾਤਿ ਰੰਗਾ ਕੇ ਨਾਵ ॥
Jeea Jaath Rangaa Kae Naav.
The living beings, of different colors and species.

ਸਭਨਾ ਲਿਖਿਆ ਵੁੜੀ ਕਲਾਮ ॥
Sabhanaa Likhiaa Vurree Kalaam.
These were all inscribed by the big pen of Creator.

ਏਹੁ ਲੇਖਾ ਲਿਖਿ ਜਾਣੈ ਕੋਇ ॥
Eaehu Laekhaa Likh Jaanai Koe.
If one wants to write this account for knowledge.

ਲੇਖਾ ਲਿਖਿਆ ਕੇਤਾ ਹੋਇ ॥
Laekhaa Likhiaa Kaethaa Hoe.
This would be such a huge scroll.

ਕੇਤਾ ਤਾਣੁ ਸੁਆਲਿਹੁ ਰੂਪੁ ॥
Kaethaa Thaan Suaalihu Roop.

What power that created the fascinating Creation.

ਕੇਤੀ ਦਾਤਿ ਜਾਣੈ ਕੌਣੁ ਕੂਤੁ ॥
Kaethee Dhaath Jaanai Kaan Kooth.
And what boons (created objects) are there. Who can know their extent?

ਕੀਤਾ ਪਸਾਉ ਏਕੋ ਕਵਾਉ ॥
Keethaa Pasaao Eaeko Kavaao.
The creation of this vast expanse is by the Shabad heard as sound (that emanates from *Ekankar*).

ਤਿਸ ਤੇ ਹੋਏ ਲਖ ਦਰੀਆਉ ॥
This Thae Hoeae Lakh Dhareeaao.
From this same sound creates Hundreds of thousands of rivers.

ਕੁਦਰਤਿ ਕਵਣ ਕਹਾ ਵੀਚਾਰੁ ॥
Kudharath Kavan Kehaa Veechaar.
How can the creativity in Nature be described?

ਵਾਰਿਆ ਨ ਜਾਵਾ ਏਕ ਵਾਰ ਜੋ ਤੁਧੁ ਭਾਵੈ ਸਾਈ ਭਲੀ ਕਾਰ ॥

ਤੂ ਸਦਾ ਸਲਾਮਤਿ ਨਿਰੰਕਾਰ ॥੧੬॥
Vaariaa N Jaavaa Eaek Vaar. Jo Thudhh Bhaavai Saaee Bhalee Kaar. Tu Sadhaa Salaamath Nirankar.
Not even once would I refrain from being devoted.
Whatever is pleases thee is the only good,
Thou are Eternal and Formless One! ||16||

Comments:

The five passions have troubled devotees a plenty. There is an element of fear behind them. When we are within the mind then through Jap takes on color of Sach. In Sach there is no fear.

Within we then do Jap dedicating all belonging to the Creator. We also this way break connection of attachment with worldly objects and affairs. These are taken to be items in trust for having experience of life. *This positive detachment is a correction. It is detachment from Haume to attachment with the Creator, the Master.*

Whenever a passion rises divert. Use this technique that shifts the state of being to Nirgun. Shift to Jap so as to let the mind thought change.

Pauri 17

ਅਸੰਖ ਜਪ ਅਸੰਖ ਭਾਉ ॥
Asankh Jap Asankh Bhaao.
Countless do meditations, countless ways to express love.

ਅਸੰਖ ਪੂਜਾ ਅਸੰਖ ਤਪ ਤਾਉ ॥
Asankh Poojaa Asankh Thap Thaao.
Countless ways of worship, countless austere disciplines.

ਅਸੰਖ ਗਰੰਥ ਮੁਖਿ ਵੇਦ ਪਾਠ ॥
Asankh Garanthh Mukh Vaedh Paath.
Countless scriptures like vedas are recited.

ਅਸੰਖ ਜੋਗ ਮਨਿ ਰਹਹਿ ਉਦਾਸ ॥
Asankh Jog Man Rehehi Oudhaas.
Countless Yogis, whose minds remain detached from the world.

ਅਸੰਖ ਭਗਤ ਗੁਣ ਗਿਆਨ ਵੀਚਾਰ ॥
Asankh Bhagath Gun Giaan Veechaar.
Countless devotees contemplate the Wisdom and Virtues of the Lord.

ਅਸੰਖ ਸਤੀ ਅਸੰਖ ਦਾਤਾਰ ॥
Asankh Sathee Asankh Dhaathaar.
Countless the holy, countless the givers.

ਅਸੰਖ ਸੂਰ ਮੁਹ ਭਖ ਸਾਰ ॥
Asankh Soor Muh Bhakh Saar.
Countless spiritual braves, who bear the difficulties.

ਅਸੰਖ ਮੋਨਿ ਲਿਵ ਲਾਇ ਤਾਰ ॥
Asankh Mon Liv Laae Taar.
Countless are sages sitting in silence, with single minded attention.

Jap Meditation Revealed

ਕੁਦਰਤਿ ਕਵਣ ਕਹਾ ਵੀਚਾਰੁ ॥
Kudharath Kavan Kehaa Veechaar.
How can the Natures expression be described?

ਵਾਰਿਆ ਨ ਜਾਵਾ ਏਕ ਵਾਰ ॥
Vaariaa N Jaavaa Eaek Vaar.
Not even once can one be capable of even once be devoted to Thee.

ਜੋ ਤੁਧੁ ਭਾਵੈ ਸਾਈ ਭਲੀ ਕਾਰ ॥
Jo Thudhh Bhaavai Saaee Bhalee Kaar.
Whatever pleases Thee is the only good deed,

ਤੂ ਸਦਾ ਸਲਾਮਤਿ ਨਿਰੰਕਾਰ ॥੧੭॥
Thoo Sadhaa Salaamath Nirankaar.
Thou are Eternal and Formless One. ||17||

Comments:

The meditation and relation with creator are personal in nature. Within the broad framework variations are there. Observe but do not copy their individual style.

Learn from the Satguru only. Believe that the words of Satguru are the Truth.

The Guru here is explaining about the diverse styles which often create doubt.

This "doubt" is most damaging in spiritual progress.

This appears to be one main reason for so much stress on being Gurmukh. The mind gets swayed by the rites and rituals. The mind wavers since Sach is not perceived immediatly. The perception has to open up first. The method is Jap with thoughts of Sach presence.

Pauri 18

ਅਸੰਖ ਮੂਰਖ ਅੰਧ ਘੋਰ ॥
Asankh Moorakh Andhh Ghor.
Countless are fools, blinded by ignorance.

ਅਸੰਖ ਚੋਰ ਹਰਾਮਖੋਰ ॥
Asankh Chor Haraamakhor.
Countless are thieves and embezzlers.

ਅਸੰਖ ਅਮਰ ਕਰਿ ਜਾਹਿ ਜੋਰ ॥
Asankh Amar Kar Jaahi Jor.
Countless are those go after a life commanding other.

ਅਸੰਖ ਗਲਵਢ ਹਤਿਆ ਕਮਾਹਿ ॥
Asankh Galavadt Hathiaa Kamaahi.
Countless are cut-throats and ruthless killers.

ਅਸੰਖ ਪਾਪੀ ਪਾਪੁ ਕਰਿ ਜਾਹਿ ॥
Asankh Paapee Paap Kar Jaahi.
Countless are sinners who keep on sinning.

ਅਸੰਖ ਕੂੜਿਆਰ ਕੂੜੇ ਫਿਰਾਹਿ ॥
Asankh Koorriaar Koorrae Fireahi.
Countless are wandering lost in the illusion of world.
ਅਸੰਖ ਮਲੇਛ ਮਲੁ ਭਖਿ ਖਾਹਿ
Asankh Malaeshh Mal Bhakh Khaahi.
Countless unethicals keep on having garbage.

ਅਸੰਖ ਨਿੰਦਕ ਸਿਰਿ ਕਰਹਿ ਭਾਰੁ ॥
Asankh Nindhak Sir Karehi Bhaar.
Countless slanderers, carrying this weight on their heads.

ਨਾਨਕੁ ਨੀਚੁ ਕਹੈ ਵੀਚਾਰੁ ॥
Nanak Neech Kehai Veechaar.
Says Nanak, seeing the state of the lowly remain in contem-

plation;

ਵਾਰਿਆ ਨ ਜਾਵਾ ਏਕ ਵਾਰ ॥
Vaariaa N Jaavaa Eaek Vaar.
Not even once can one be capable of even once be devoted to Thee.

ਜੋ ਤੁਧੁ ਭਾਵੈ ਸਾਈ ਭਲੀ ਕਾਰ ॥
Jo Thudhh Bhaavai Saaee Bhalee Kaar.
Whatever pleases Thee is the only good deed,

ਤੂ ਸਦਾ ਸਲਾਮਤਿ ਨਿਰੰਕਾਰ ॥੧੮॥
Thoo Sadhaa Salaamath Nirankar.
Thou are Eternal and Formless One. ||18||

Comments:

This here is about ignorance. The world and the actions of others attract. We tend to follow the same worldly ways. This here is time that requires steadfastness and belief. Follow only the Gurbani way.

Pauri 19

ਅਸੰਖ ਨਾਵ ਅਸੰਖ ਥਾਵ ॥
Asankh Naav Asankh Thhaav.
Countless are thy names, countless are thy places.

ਅਗੰਮ ਅਗੰਮ ਅਸੰਖ ਲੋਅ ॥
Agam Agam Asankh Loa.
Countless are inaccessible, unapproachable created realms.

ਅਸੰਖ ਕਹਹਿ ਸਿਰਿ ਭਾਰੁ ਹੋਇ ॥
Asankh Kehehi Sir Bhaar Hoe.
Saying these countless names would prove heavy for the head.

ਅਖਰੀ ਨਾਮੁ ਅਖਰੀ ਸਾਲਾਹ ॥
Akharee Naam Akharee Saalaah.
The words are used for Naam, words comprise the hymns for glorious singing.

ਅਖਰੀ ਗਿਆਨੁ ਗੀਤ ਗੁਣ ਗਾਹ ॥
Akharee Giaan Geeth Gun Gaah.
The words are used in giving and receiving knowledge and the hymns that are sung telling the characteristic Sach qualities.

ਅਖਰੀ ਲਿਖਣੁ ਬੋਲਣੁ ਬਾਣਿ ॥
Akharee Likhan Bolan Baan.
With words is done speech and writing.

ਅਖਰਾ ਸਿਰਿ ਸੰਜੋਗੁ ਵਖਾਣਿ ॥
Akharaa Sir Sanjog Vakhaan.
The words are thoughts in our head that write the destiny.
(As are our thoughts so are our circumstances and situations)

ਜਿਨਿ ਏਹਿ ਲਿਖੇ ਤਿਸੁ ਸਿਰਿ ਨਾਹਿ ॥

Jin Eaehi Likhae This Sir Naahi.
But the One who made this system of destiny has no form with head and neither has any destiny.

ਜਿਵ ਫੁਰਮਾਏ ਤਿਵ ਤਿਵ ਪਾਹਿ ॥
Jiv Furamaaeae Thiv Thiv Paahi.
As it is ordained (Hukam), so do we receive
(via karmic cause and effect).

ਜੇਤਾ ਕੀਤਾ ਤੇਤਾ ਨਾਉ ॥
Jaethaa Keethaa Thaethaa Naao.
All that is created is the manifestation of Naam.

ਵਿਣੁ ਨਾਵੈ ਨਾਹੀ ਕੋ ਥਾਉ ॥
Vin Naavai Naahee Ko Thhaao.
Without the Naam, there is no place that exists.

ਕੁਦਰਤਿ ਕਵਣ ਕਹਾ ਵੀਚਾਰੁ ॥
Kudharath Kavan Kehaa Veechaar.
Observe the working of nature, contemplate on these.
(There is *Hukam* in working of Nature. It is to be observed by feeling the presence. The workings of Hukam indicates Creator.)

ਵਾਰਿਆ ਨ ਜਾਵਾ ਏਕ ਵਾਰ ॥
Vaariaa N Jaavaa Eaek Vaar.
Not even once can one be capable of even once be devoted to Thee.

ਜੋ ਤੁਧੁ ਭਾਵੈ ਸਾਈ ਭਲੀ ਕਾਰ ॥
Jo Thudhh Bhaavai Saaee Bhalee Kaar.
Whatever pleases You is the only good deed,

ਤੂ ਸਦਾ ਸਲਾਮਤਿ ਨਿਰੰਕਾਰ ॥੧੯॥
Thoo Sadhaa Salaamath Nirankaar.
Thou are Eternal and Formless One. ||19||

Comments:

First, the Names are countless with their origin too from countless places. So, these cannot be the basis for Jap.

Second, that the Naam is present in all places. Nowhere and nothing is without Naam. In Nature is seen expressions of Naam - HIS presence. The workings of Nature have a power and system indicating unseen presence of Naam. Contemplating and on observing of these expressions indicate the presence of Naam.

Third, the thoughts in our mind, which are words too, define our course of life. This is karmic system, as we would see later and dynamic in nature. The Creator however is out of any such system.

Pauri 20

ਭਰੀਐ ਹਥੁ ਪੈਰੁ ਤਨੁ ਦੇਹ
Bhareeai Hathh Pair Than Dhaeh.
When the hands and the feet and the body are dirty,

ਪਾਣੀ ਧੋਤੈ ਉਤਰਸੁ ਖੇਹ ॥
Paanee Dhhothai Outharas Khaeh.
Water can wash away the dirt.

ਮੂਤ ਪਲੀਤੀ ਕਪੜੁ ਹੋਇ ॥
Mooth Paleethee Kaparr Hoe.
When the clothes are soiled and stained by urine,

ਦੇ ਸਾਬੂਣੁ ਲਈਐ ਓਹੁ ਧੋਇ ॥
Dhae Saaboon Leeai Ouhu Dhhoe.
Soap can wash them clean.

ਭਰੀਐ ਮਤਿ ਪਾਪਾ ਕੈ ਸੰਗਿ ॥
Bhareeai Math Paapaa Kai Sang.
Do not fill the intellect with the sin,

ਓਹੁ ਧੋਪੈ ਨਾਵੈ ਕੈ ਰੰਗਿ ॥
Ouhu Dhhopai Naavai Kai Rang.
It then can be cleansed only by the color imbued by Naam.

ਪੁੰਨੀ ਪਾਪੀ ਆਖਣੁ ਨਾਹਿ ॥
Punnee Paapee Aakhan Naahi.
The sinner cannot become virtuous by mere words;
  (Just saying you have pure heart does not make you clean. Neither can you express good in all conduct.)

ਕਰਿ ਕਰਿ ਕਰਣਾ ਲਿਖਿ ਲੈ ਜਾਹੁ ॥
Kar Kar Karanaa Likh Lai Jaahu.
In life actions repeated, over and over again, are engraved and even carried over to next lives.

ਆਪੇ ਬੀਜਿ ਆਪੇ ਹੀ ਖਾਹੁ ॥
Aapae Beej Aapae Hee Khaahu.
What is sown by own self is what one gets to eat.

ਨਾਨਕ ਹੁਕਮੀ ਆਵਹੁ ਜਾਹੁ ॥੨੦॥
Nanak Hukamee Aavahu Jaahu.
Says Nanak, this is the way of the Hukam that, due to these actions we come and go in reincarnation. ||20||

Comments:
Our minds adapt to the color of thoughts. Our involvement in this world fills our mind with Haume driven attachments, negative behavior patterns, fear and anxiety.

The karmic system is clear: as we sow so we reap. The spiritual efforts do also bear karmic results.

The karma that is done the Gurbani way takes you out of Karma. The Naam is a purity. It comes and colors the mind.

This happens when one is detaches Haume. The Haume is not their when Karta's is in Conscious Awareness. Both of them are not together as Haume is a created existence. Shift Haume's attachments to Karta and Haume ceases to exist. This is the way to let haume die in conscious awareness.

Another important point to remember for "Color of Naam" to come is to go within and stay at the Nirgun point hearing the Shabad, even with eyes open.

Pauri 21

ਤੀਰਥੁ ਤਪੁ ਦਇਆ ਦਤੁ ਦਾਨੁ ॥
Thirath Tapp Dhiyaa Dhath Dhaan.
Pilgrimages, austere discipline, compassion and charity are being done.

ਜੇ ਕੋ ਪਾਵੈ ਤਿਲ ਕਾ ਮਾਨੁ ॥
Jae Ko Paavai Thil Kaa Maan.
But If one wants even an iota of honor, then –

ਸੁਣਿਆ ਮੰਨਿਆ ਮਨਿ ਕੀਤਾ ਭਾਉ ॥
Suniya Manniaa Mann Keethaa Bhaao.
Listening (Naam), having acceptance and love in the mind-

ਅੰਤਰਗਤਿ ਤੀਰਥਿ ਮਲਿ ਨਾਉ ॥
Antharagath Theerathh Mal Naao.
Then within one has the bath of pilgrimage that cleanses.

ਸਭਿ ਗੁਣ ਤੇਰੇ ਮੈ ਨਾਹੀ ਕੋਇ ॥
Sabh Gun Thaerae Mai Naahee Koe.
All virtues are Yours, whereas my identity has none.

ਵਿਣੁ ਗੁਣ ਕੀਤੇ ਭਗਤਿ ਨ ਹੋਇ ॥
Vin Gun Keethae Bhagath N Hoe.
Without virtue, there is no devotional worship.

ਸੁਅਸਤਿ ਆਥਿ ਬਾਣੀ ਬਰਮਾਉ ॥
Suasatt Aathh Baani Baramaao.
Within is received a benefit (Suasatt) which is hearing of the sound (Baani) that created (Baramaao) creation.

ਸਤਿ ਸੁਹਾਣੁ ਸਦਾ ਮਨਿ ਚਾਉ ॥
Satt Suhaan Sadhaa Man Chaao.
The Satt (that which is true) is ever pleasing, and the mind yearns for it.

ਕਵਣੁ ਸੁ ਵੇਲਾ ਵਖਤੁ ਕਵਣੁ ਕਵਣ ਥਿਤਿ ਕਵਣੁ ਵਾਰੁ ॥
Kavan S Vaelaa Vakhath Kavan Kavan Thith Kavan Vaar.
What was that time, and what was that moment? What was that day, and what was that date?

ਕਵਣਿ ਸਿ ਰੁਤੀ ਮਾਹੁ ਕਵਣੁ ਜਿਤੁ ਹੋਆ ਆਕਾਰੁ ॥
Kavan S Ruthee Maahu Kavan Jith Hoaa Aakaar.
What was that season, and what was that month, when the form was created?

ਵੇਲ ਨ ਪਾਈਆ ਪੰਡਤੀ ਜਿ ਹੋਵੈ ਲੇਖੁ ਪੁਰਾਣੁ ॥
Vael N Paaeeaa Panddathee J Hovai Laekh Puraan.
The Pandits, the religious scholars, cannot find that time, even if it is written in the Puranas (old scriptures).

ਵਖਤੁ ਨ ਪਾਇਓ ਕਾਦੀਆ ਜਿ ਲਿਖਨਿ ਲੇਖੁ ਕੁਰਾਣੁ ॥
Vakhath N Paeiou Kadheeaa J Likhan Laekh Kuraan.
That time is not known to the Qazis, who study the Koran.

ਥਿਤਿ ਵਾਰੁ ਨਾ ਜੋਗੀ ਜਾਣੈ ਰੁਤਿ ਮਾਹੁ ਨਾ ਕੋਈ ॥
Thhith Vaar Naa Jogee Jaanai Ruth Maahu Naa Koee.
The day, date and season are not known to the Yogis.

ਜਾ ਕਰਤਾ ਸਿਰਠੀ ਕਉ ਸਾਜੇ ਆਪੇ ਜਾਣੈ ਸੋਈ ॥
Jaa Karathaa Sirathee Ko Saajae Aapae Jaanai Soee.
The Creator who created this creation-only knows.

ਕਿਵ ਕਰਿ ਆਖਾ ਕਿਵ ਸਾਲਾਹੀ ਕਿਉ ਵਰਨੀ ਕਿਵ ਜਾਣਾ ॥
Kiv Kar Aakhaa Kiv Salahee Kio Varanee Kiv Jaanaa.
In what way should we speak of HIM? How can we praise HIM? How can we describe HIM? How can we know HIM?

ਨਾਨਕ ਆਖਣਿ ਸਭੁ ਕੋ ਆਖੈ ਇਕ ਦੂ ਇਕੁ ਸਿਆਣਾ ॥
Nanak Aakhan Sabh Ko Aakhai Eik Dhoo Eik Siaanaa
Says Nanak, everyone speaks of Him, each one wiser than the rest.

ਵਡਾ ਸਾਹਿਬੁ ਵਡੀ ਨਾਈ ਕੀਤਾ ਜਾ ਕਾ ਹੋਵੈ ॥

Vaddaa Saahib Vaddee Naaee Keethaa Jaa Kaa Hovai. Great is the Master, Great is HIS Name. Whatever is happening is HIS Will.

ਨਾਨਕ ਜੇ ਕੋ ਆਪੌ ਜਾਣੈ ਅਗੈ ਗਇਆ ਨ ਸੋਹੈ ॥੨੧॥

Nanak Jae Ko Aapa Jaanai Agai Gaeiaa N Sohai ||21|| Says Nanak, one who believes in self greatness, shall not go further. ||21||

Comments:

It is when we shift from Sargun world and go within that the real worship and pilgrimage begins.

The language is of love. It is through feeling that one connects with the formless. The Guru here points out a truth that all that is happening is the play of Hukam.

The Haume however makes one swell in ego thinking otherwise. These people do not go further. The hint is to detach from the Haume.

The Jap is to see the working of Hukam in everything. This truth needs to be contemplated as Jap. (By contemplation is meant thinking, observing, asking how, reading about.)

Jap is that "All virtues are Yours, whereas my identity has none." Think- HE is talking, walking, driving, working, playing. HE is the Player inside and outside in creation.

With *Haume* not in play, the treasure is received within. For this Jap of "HIM being all that is" needed to be done. The Anhad Shabad, the Celestial sound of creation then begins to be heard. This *Shabad* creates the five elements. There are distinct sounds for them. This sound is present in every being.

Pauri 22

ਪਾਤਾਲਾ ਪਾਤਾਲ ਲਖ ਆਗਾਸਾ ਆਗਾਸ ॥
Paatala Paataal Lakh Aagasa Aagaas.
There are nether worlds beneath nether worlds, and hundreds of thousands of worlds in Sky (space).

ਉੜਕ ਉੜਕ ਭਾਲਿ ਥਕੇ ਵੇਦ ਕਹਨਿ ਇਕ ਵਾਤ ॥
Ourrak Ourrak Bhaal Thhakae Vaedh Kehan Eik Vaath.
This one can search and search, until one grows weary; about them Veda's say-

ਸਹਸ ਅਠਾਰਹ ਕਹਨਿ ਕਤੇਬਾ ਅਸੁਲੂ ਇਕੁ ਧਾਤੁ ॥
Sehas Athaareh Kehan Kathaebaa Asuloo Eik Dhhaath.
The scriptures say that there are 18,000 worlds, but in reality, there is only One essence (the base).

ਲੇਖਾ ਹੋਇ ਤ ਲਿਖੀਐ ਲੇਖੈ ਹੋਇ ਵਿਣਾਸੁ ॥
Laekhaa Hoe Th Likheeai Laekhai Hoe Vinaas.
If you try to write an account of this, you will surely finish yourself before you finish writing it.

ਨਾਨਕ ਵਡਾ ਆਖੀਐ ਆਪੇ ਜਾਣੈ ਆਪੁ ॥੨੨॥
Nanak Vaddaa Aakheeai Aapae Jaanai Aap.
Says Nanak, all call HIM Great. But only HE HIMSELF can know HIMSELF. ||22||

Comments:

This Pauri talks of existence of millions of worlds both subtle and in space. These are limitless and we would be incapable of knowing let alone describing. These would be having created beings quite different and with a different set of thoughts.

Our position among this ocean of universes is very very small. We simply are becoming a drop in the ocean.

Some scriptures talk of 18000 worlds or some would be giving a different count. The Guru takes us away from these counts and asks us to remember that the essence is same. (Earlier the Guru has clarified that these are countless.)

In fact, the same is also our nature. The Mool is same. What is in the universe is within us too. This statement means we are part of the thread of oneness. Whether ocean or a drop both are water.

The mentioning of these counts is important in that there can be no limit to the extent of creations. We should not accept as true the statements in some literature. Our focus is not knowledge about them but the Creator.

This thinking would be a diversion. This is the manner in which *Maya* (the deception, illusion) works.

Pauri 23

ਸਾਲਾਹੀ ਸਾਲਾਹਿ ਏਤੀ ਸੁਰਤਿ ਨ ਪਾਈਆ ॥
Saalahee Saalah Eaethee Surat N Paeaa.
The praisers praise, but their awareness does not fathom the vastness;

ਨਦੀਆ ਅਤੈ ਵਾਹ ਪਵਹਿ ਸਮੁੰਦਿ ਨ ਜਾਣੀਅਹਿ ॥
Nadheeaa Athai Vaah Pavehi Samundh N Jaaneeahi.
Like the streams and rivers flowing into the ocean do not known its vastness.

ਸਮੁੰਦ ਸਾਹ ਸੁਲਤਾਨ ਗਿਰਹਾ ਸੇਤੀ ਮਾਲੁ ਧਨੁ ॥
Samundh Saah Sulathaan Girehaa Saethee Maal Dhhan.
Even by being a king, emperor, with mountains of wealth and belongings.

ਕੀੜੀ ਤੁਲਿ ਨ ਹੋਵਨੀ ਜੇ ਤਿਸੁ ਮਨਹੁ ਨ ਵੀਸਰਹਿ ॥੨੩॥
Keerree Thul N Hovanee Jae This Manahu N Veesarehi.
Does not equal an ant, which does not forget God.

Comments:

Forgetting being a haume driven being and instead having "oneness in presence" is far greater than having wealth and position on earth.

Pauri 24

ਅੰਤੁ ਨ ਸਿਫਤੀ ਕਹਣਿ ਨ ਅੰਤੁ ॥
Anth N Sifathee Kehan N Anth.
Endless are the Praises, endless are those who speak these.

ਅੰਤੁ ਨ ਕਰਣੈ ਦੇਣਿ ਨ ਅੰਤੁ ॥
Anth N Karanai Dhaen N Anth.
Endless are the creations, endless are the given Gifts.

ਅੰਤੁ ਨ ਵੇਖਣਿ ਸੁਣਨਿ ਨ ਅੰਤੁ ॥
Anth N Vaekhan Sunan N Anth.
Endless is all that is being seen, endless is what is heard.

ਅੰਤੁ ਨ ਜਾਪੈ ਕਿਆ ਮਨਿ ਮੰਤੁ ॥
Anth N Jaapai Kiaa Man Manth.
There is no end to virtues in the mind.

ਅੰਤੁ ਨ ਜਾਪੈ ਕੀਤਾ ਆਕਾਰੁ ॥
Anth N Jaapai Keethaa Aakaar.
The limits of the created universe cannot be perceived.

ਅੰਤੁ ਨ ਜਾਪੈ ਪਾਰਾਵਾਰੁ ॥
Anth N Jaapai Paaraavaar.
Its limits here and beyond cannot be perceived.

ਅੰਤ ਕਾਰਣਿ ਕੇਤੇ ਬਿਲਲਾਹਿ ॥
Anth Kaaran Kaethae Bilalaahi.
Many struggles to know the limits.

ਤਾ ਕੇ ਅੰਤ ਨ ਪਾਏ ਜਾਹਿ ॥
Thaa Kae Anth N Paaeae Jaahi.
But the limits cannot be found.

ਏਹੁ ਅੰਤੁ ਨ ਜਾਣੈ ਕੋਇ ॥
Eaehu Anth N Jaanai Koe.

No one can know these limits.

ਬਹੁਤਾ ਕਹੀਐ ਬਹੁਤਾ ਹੋਇ ॥
Bahuthaa Keheeai Bahuthaa Hoe.
The more one says about them,
the more there is still remaining to be said.

ਵਡਾ ਸਾਹਿਬੁ ਊਚਾ ਥਾਉ ॥
Vaddaa Saahib Oochaa Thhaao.
Immense is the Master, and high is the HIS place.

ਊਚੇ ਉਪਰਿ ਊਚਾ ਨਾਉ ॥
Oochae Oupar Oochaa Naao.
That high is reached only through HIS high Naam.

ਏਵਡੁ ਊਚਾ ਹੋਵੈ ਕੋਇ ॥
Eaevadd Oochaa Hovai Koe.
Only way is to reach that high.

ਤਿਸੁ ਊਚੇ ਕਉ ਜਾਣੈ ਸੋਇ ॥
Tis Oochae Ko Jaanai Soe.
Then one does know the high Master.

ਜੇਵਡੁ ਆਪਿ ਜਾਣੈ ਆਪਿ ਆਪਿ ॥
Jaevadd Aap Jaanai Aap Aap.
About HIM only HE HIMSELF knows.

ਨਾਨਕ ਨਦਰੀ ਕਰਮੀ ਦਾਤਿ ॥੨੪॥
Nanak Nadharee Karamee Dhaath.
Says Nanak, by karmic actions, the Nadar (vision of awareness) is bestowed. ||24||

Comments:

The Guru is explaining the immenseness of the creation which only indicates how exalted is the Creator.

Knowing and feeling this is spiritually important. The Jap (regular reading) of this Baani (composition) is needed so that our mind begins the acceptances process. Otherwise there is doubt, the mind skips and we would remain ignorant.

In the world it can be observed that there is tendency to limit the creator. This is done by giving HIM a human form with super power, considering HIM to be present at some place, image or an idol.

Through Jap we have to come out of any influence of these worship methods that show limits. The Creator is immense limitless and is everywhere in creation.

Pauri 25

ਬਹੁਤਾ ਕਰਮੁ ਲਿਖਿਆ ਨਾ ਜਾਇ ॥
Bahuthaa Karam Likhiaa Naa Jaae.
Many of our positive appearing karma are not spiritual.

ਵਡਾ ਦਾਤਾ ਤਿਲੁ ਨ ਤਮਾਇ ॥
Vaddaa Dhaathaa Til N Thamaae.
The Great Giver does not have an iota of need.

ਕੇਤੇ ਮੰਗਹਿ ਜੋਧ ਅਪਾਰ ॥
Kaethae Mangehi Jodhh Apaar.
There are so many great warriors begging from HIM.

ਕੇਤਿਆ ਗਣਤ ਨਹੀ ਵੀਚਾਰੁ ॥
Kaethiaa Ganath Nehee Veechaar.
So many contemplate and dwell to know about HIM.

ਕੇਤੇ ਖਪਿ ਤੁਟਹਿ ਵੇਕਾਰ ॥
Kaethae Khap Thuttehi Vaekaar.
So many wastes away life engaged in vices.

ਕੇਤੇ ਲੈ ਲੈ ਮੁਕਰੁ ਪਾਹਿ ॥
Kaethae Lai Lai Mukar Paahi.
So many receive again and then forget the giver.

ਕੇਤੇ ਮੂਰਖ ਖਾਹੀ ਖਾਹਿ ॥ ਕੇਤਿਆ ਦੂਖ ਭੂਖ ਸਦ ਮਾਰ ॥
Kaethae Moorakh Khaahee Khaahi. Kaethiaa Dhookh Bhookh Sadh Maar.
So many foolish who keep on living in comforts.
While so many endure distress, deprivation and abuse.

ਏਹਿ ਭਿ ਦਾਤਿ ਤੇਰੀ ਦਾਤਾਰ ॥
Eaehi Bh Dhaath Thaeree Dhaathaar.
Even these are gifts which makes you spiritual.

ਬੰਦਿ ਖਲਾਸੀ ਭਾਣੈ ਹੋਇ ॥
Bandh Khalaasee Bhaanai Hoe.
Liberation from bondage comes only by right action.

ਹੋਰੁ ਆਖਿ ਨ ਸਕੈ ਕੋਇ ॥
Hor Aakh N Sakai Koe.
No one else has any say in this.

ਜੇ ਕੋ ਖਾਇਕੁ ਆਖਣਿ ਪਾਇ ॥
Jae Ko Khaaeik Aakhan Paae.
If some fool should presume to say that he does,

ਓਹੁ ਜਾਣੈ ਜੇਤੀਆ ਮੁਹਿ ਖਾਇ ॥
Ouhu Jaanai Jaetheeaa Muhi Khaae.
He shall learn, and feel the effects of his folly.

ਆਪੇ ਜਾਣੈ ਆਪੇ ਦੇਇ ॥
Aapae Jaanai Aapae Dhaee.
HE Himself knows, HE Himself gives.
ਆਖਹਿ ਸਿ ਭਿ ਕੇਈ ਕੇਇ ॥
Aakhehi S Bh Kaeee Kaee.
Few, very few are those who ask in this way.

ਜਿਸ ਨੋ ਬਖਸੇ ਸਿਫਤਿ ਸਾਲਾਹ ॥ ਨਾਨਕ ਪਾਤਿਸਾਹੀ ਪਾਤਿਸਾਹੁ ॥੨੫॥
Jis No Bakhsae Sift Salaah. Nanak Pathsahee Paatisaah.
To those HE blesses with Sift Salah (devotion).
Says Nanak, they are the king of kings. ||25||

Comments:

Some adopt a devotional method like offerings, trade, prayers and feel entitled to be blessed. These actions are not devotional service. The suffering too are gift as these work like medicine. They then learn right devotional service.

Pauri 26

ਅਮੁਲ ਗੁਣ ਅਮੁਲ ਵਾਪਾਰ ॥
Amul Gun Amul Vaapaar.
Priceless are HIS Virtues, Priceless is the trade (the Jap).
ਅਮੁਲ ਵਾਪਾਰੀਏ ਅਮੁਲ ਭੰਡਾਰ ॥
Amul Vaapaareeeae Amul Bhanddaar.
Priceless are the Traders (of Jap), Priceless is the Treasure (benifits).

ਅਮੁਲ ਆਵਹਿ ਅਮੁਲ ਲੈ ਜਾਹਿ ॥
Amul Aavehi Amul Lai Jaahi.
Priceless are those who come (to learn of these), Priceless are those who buy (follow).

ਅਮੁਲ ਭਾਇ ਅਮੁਲਾ ਸਮਾਹਿ ॥
Amul Bhaae Amulaa Samaahi.
Priceless is Love, Priceless is absorption with it.

ਅਮੁਲੁ ਧਰਮੁ ਅਮੁਲੁ ਦੀਬਾਣੁ ॥
Amul Dhharam Amul Dheebaan.
Priceless is the Dharma, Priceless is the Divine Court.

ਅਮੁਲੁ ਤੁਲੁ ਅਮੁਲੁ ਪਰਵਾਣੁ ॥
Amul Tul Amul Paravaan.
Priceless is the scale (karmic law) that chooses, priceless is the acceptance.

ਅਮੁਲੁ ਬਖਸੀਸ ਅਮੁਲੁ ਨੀਸਾਣੁ ॥
Amul Bakhasees Amul Neesaan.
Priceless is the Blessing, Priceless the indications.
ਅਮੁਲੁ ਕਰਮੁ ਅਮੁਲੁ ਫੁਰਮਾਣੁ ॥
Amul Karam Amul Furmaan.
Priceless are the right karma, Priceless is the Hukam.

ਅਮੁਲੋ ਅਮੁਲੁ ਆਖਿਆ ਨ ਜਾਇ ॥
Amulo Amul Aakhiaa N Jaae.
So priceless is obediance that it cannot be expressed.

ਆਖਿ ਆਖਿ ਰਹੇ ਲਿਵ ਲਾਇ ॥
Aakh Aakh Rehae Liv Laae.
Saying again and again (Jap), they remain absorbed.

ਆਖਹਿ ਵੇਦ ਪਾਠ ਪੁਰਾਣ ॥
Aakhehi Vaedh Paath Puraan.
Many speak of reading Vedas and the Puranas.

ਆਖਹਿ ਪੜੇ ਕਰਹਿ ਵਖਿਆਣ ॥
Aakhehi Parrae Karehi Vakhiaan.
Many philosophers study then describe.

ਆਖਹਿ ਬਰਮੇ ਆਖਹਿ ਇੰਦ ॥
Aakhehi Baramae Aakhehi Eindh.
Many speak of the Brahma and the Indra.

ਆਖਹਿ ਗੋਪੀ ਤੈ ਗੋਵਿੰਦ ॥
Aakhehi Gopee Thai Govindh.
Many others speak of the Gopis and Krishna.

ਆਖਹਿ ਈਸਰ ਆਖਹਿ ਸਿਧ ॥
Aakhehi Eesar Aakhehi Sidhh.
Many speak of Ishvar (God) and of becoming Siddh.

ਆਖਹਿ ਕੇਤੇ ਕੀਤੇ ਬੁਧ ॥
Aakhehi Kaethae Keethae Budhh.
Many speak of becoming like Buddhas.

ਆਖਹਿ ਦਾਨਵ ਆਖਹਿ ਦੇਵ ॥
Aakhehi Dhaanav Aakhehi Dhaev.
Many speak of the demons and the devas.

ਆਖਹਿ ਸੁਰਿ ਨਰ ਮੁਨਿ ਜਨ ਸੇਵ ॥
Aakhehi Sur Nar Mun Jan Saev.
Many speak about the Seers, the silent sages and their way of service.

ਕੇਤੇ ਆਖਹਿ ਆਖਣਿ ਪਾਹਿ ॥
Kaethae Aakhehi Aakhan Paahi.
Many speak and try to describe HIM.

ਕੇਤੇ ਕਹਿ ਕਹਿ ਉਠਿ ਉਠਿ ਜਾਹਿ ॥
Kaethae Kehi Kehi Outh Outh Jaahi.
Many who have spoken of HIM, have departed.

ਏਤੇ ਕੀਤੇ ਹੋਰਿ ਕਰੇਹਿ ॥
Eaethae Keethae Hor Karaehi.
Many beings were created as and many would again.

ਤਾ ਆਖਿ ਨ ਸਕਹਿ ਕੇਈ ਕੇਇ ॥
Thaa Aakh N Sakehi Kaeee Kaee.
Even then, they cannot not describe HIM.

ਜੇਵਡੁ ਭਾਵੈ ਤੇਵਡੁ ਹੋਇ ॥
Jaevadd Bhaavai Thaevadd Hoe.
Whatso ever pleases HIM, so does that come to happen.

ਨਾਨਕ ਜਾਣੈ ਸਾਚਾ ਸੋਇ ॥
Nanak Jaanai Saachaa Soe.
Says Nanak, only the True Lord knows.

ਜੇ ਕੋ ਆਖੈ ਬੋਲੁਵਿਗਾੜੁ ॥
Jae Ko Aakhai Bolvigaar.
If anyone presumes to know and describe God,

ਤਾ ਲਿਖੀਐ ਸਿਰਿ ਗਾਵਾਰਾ ਗਾਵਾਰੁ ॥੨੬॥
Taa Likheeai Sirr Gavaraa Gavaar ||26||
Then they are destined to be known as the greatest of fools. ||26||

Comments:

The devotional service is priceless. The right one is a blessing. When a devotee is on this path then many ways spoken by others appear attractive. Some even use big words to describe the exalted immense stature of the Creator. In different ways they tell.

The perception of truth and description of Creator varies. It must be kept in mind always that no one can fully know nor described the Creator. Anyone who claims so is a fool.

In this world there is mix of purity with impurity - creator and created. Only the Naam is true which is so subtle that its experience comes through Nadar (vision of awareness).

To follow the Guru and remaining steadfast avoiding diversions of fine interpretations is being hinted by the Guru. If these pauries are recited as Jap with meaning in mind then a different attitude develops.

Pauri 27

ਸੋ ਦਰੁ ਕੇਹਾ ਸੋ ਘਰੁ ਕੇਹਾ ਜਿਤੁ ਬਹਿ ਸਰਬ ਸਮਾਲੇ ॥
Jith Behi Sarab Samaalae.
Where is the path that leads to the Dwelling, in where while sitting is taking care of everything?

ਵਾਜੇ ਨਾਦ ਅਨੇਕ ਅਸੰਖਾ ਕੇਤੇ ਵਾਵਣਹਾਰੇ ॥
Vaajae Naad Anaek Asankhaa Kaethae Vavanhare.
The Naad is resounding and countless are musicians (go within and listen).

ਕੇਤੇ ਰਾਗ ਪਰੀ ਸਿਉ ਕਹੀਅਨਿ ਕੇਤੇ ਗਾਵਣਹਾਰੇ ॥
Kaethae Raag Paree Sio Keheean Kaethae Gavanhare.
There are many Ragas and Ragnees (many life forms) and many are the singers (worshipers).

ਗਾਵਹਿ ਤੁਹਨੋ ਪਉਣੁ ਪਾਣੀ ਬੈਸੰਤਰੁ ਗਾਵੈ ਰਾਜਾ ਧਰਮੁ ਦੁਆਰੇ ॥
Gaavehi Tuhno Pawan Paanee Baisanthar Gaavai Raajaa Dhharam Dhuaarae.
They too sing who are in air (their actions are in ego), water (their actions have purity) or fire (their actions are aggresive) and sing about the King Judge of Dharma sitting on door (actually the karma decides who can enter court).

ਗਾਵਹਿ ਚਿਤੁ ਗੁਪਤੁ ਲਿਖਿ ਜਾਣਹਿ ਲਿਖਿ ਲਿਖਿ ਧਰਮੁ ਵੀਚਾਰੇ ॥
Gaavehi Chith Gupath Likh Jaanehi Likh Likh Dhharam Veechaarae.
They sing that the Chitra Gupt, (mythical name for the subconscious recording of all our actions) which are judged based on Dharma. (The core memory records with beliefs is the mythical name - Chitra Gupt)

ਗਾਵਹਿ ਈਸਰੁ ਬਰਮਾ ਦੇਵੀ ਸੋਹਨਿ ਸਦਾ ਸਵਾਰੇ ॥
Gaavehi Eesar Baramaa Dhaevee Sohan Sadhaa Savaarae.
They sing about the Ishvar, Brahma and the beautiful Goddess, who make smooth the life.

ਗਾਵਹਿ ਇੰਦ ਇਦਾਸਣਿ ਬੈਠੇ ਦੇਵਤਿਆ ਦਰਿ ਨਾਲੇ ॥
Gaavehi Eindh Eidhaasan Baithae Dhaevathiaa Dhar Naalae.
They sing of the God Indra sitting along with the Goddesses, at the Door.

ਗਾਵਹਿ ਸਿਧ ਸਮਾਧੀ ਅੰਦਰਿ ਗਾਵਨਿ ਸਾਧ ਵਿਚਾਰੇ ॥
Gaavehi Sidhh Samaadhhee Andhar Gaavan Saadhh Vichaarae.
They sing about the Siddhas in Samadhi; and about the Sadhus in contemplation.

ਗਾਵਨਿ ਜਤੀ ਸਤੀ ਸੰਤੋਖੀ ਗਾਵਹਿ ਵੀਰ ਕਰਾਰੇ ॥
Gaavan Jat-hee Sat-hee Santhokhee Gaavehi Veer Kararae.
They sing about the brave act of celibates, the chaste and the contended.

ਗਾਵਨਿ ਪੰਡਿਤ ਪੜਨਿ ਰਖੀਸਰ ਜੁਗੁ ਜੁਗੁ ਵੇਦਾ ਨਾਲੇ ॥
Gaavan Pandit Parran Rakhisar Jug Jug Vaida Nalae.
The sing of the Pandits (the religious scholars), sages who are recite the Vedas in all ages.

ਗਾਵਹਿ ਮੋਹਣੀਆ ਮਨੁ ਮੋਹਨਿ ਸੁਰਗਾ ਮਛ ਪਇਆਲੇ ॥
Gaaveh Mohanea Mann-Mohan Surga Machh Peiale.
They sing about the Mohinis (the enchanting beauties) who entice .

ਗਾਵਨਿ ਰਤਨ ਉਪਾਏ ਤੇਰੇ ਅਠਸਠਿ ਤੀਰਥ ਨਾਲੇ ॥
Gaavan Rathan Oupaaeae Thaerae Athasath Theerathh Naalae.
Some sing about the sixty-eight holy places of pilgrimage which are created to be like jewels.

ਗਾਵਹਿ ਜੋਧ ਮਹਾਬਲ ਸੂਰਾ ਗਾਵਹਿ ਖਾਣੀ ਚਾਰੇ ॥
Gaavehi Jodh Mehabal Suraa Gaavehi Khanee Chaare.
They sing about the brave and mighty warriors who also have come out of the four sources of creation.

ਗਾਵਹਿ ਖੰਡ ਮੰਡਲ ਵਰਭੰਡਾ ਕਰਿ ਕਰਿ ਰਖੇ ਧਾਰੇ ॥
Gaavehi Khand Manddal Varabhanddaa Kar Kar Rakhae Dhhaarae.
They sing HE created planets, solar systems and galaxies.

ਸੇਈ ਤੁਧੁਨੋ ਗਾਵਹਿ ਜੋ ਤੁਧੁ ਭਾਵਨਿ ਰਤੇ ਤੇਰੇ ਭਗਤ ਰਸਾਲੇ ॥
Saeee Thudhhuno Gaavehi Jo Thudhh Bhaavan Rathae Thaerae Bhagath Rasaalae ||
They alone sing, who are pleasing to thee. The devotees are imbued with the Nectar of Your Essence.

ਹੋਰਿ ਕੇਤੇ ਗਾਵਨਿ ਸੇ ਮੈ ਚਿਤਿ ਨ ਆਵਨਿ ਨਾਨਕੁ ਕਿਆ ਵੀਚਾਰੇ ॥
Hor Kaete Gaavan Sae Mai Chit N Aavan Nanak Kiaa Vicharae.
So many others sing about their ways, they do not come to mind. Says Nanak, how can we consider them all.

ਸੋਈ ਸੋਈ ਸਦਾ ਸਚੁ ਸਾਹਿਬੁ ਸਾਚਾ ਸਾਚੀ ਨਾਈ ॥
Soee Soee Sadhaa Sach Sahib Sachaa Sachee Naaee.
The True Lord is True, Forever True, and True is the Naam.

ਹੈ ਭੀ ਹੋਸੀ ਜਾਇ ਨ ਜਾਸੀ ਰਚਨਾ ਜਿਨਿ ਰਚਾਈ ॥
Hai Bhee Hosee Jaae N Jaasee Rachanaa Jin Rachaaee.
HE who Created shall always be. HE would remain, even when this created Universe departs.

ਰੰਗੀ ਰੰਗੀ ਭਾਤੀ ਕਰਿ ਕਰਿ ਜਿਨਸੀ ਮਾਇਆ ਜਿਨਿ ਉਪਾਈ ॥
Rangee Rangee Bhaatee Kar Kar Jinasee Maaeiaa Jin Oupaaee.

HE created the world, with its various colours, species of beings, and the variety of Maya.
ਕਰਿ ਕਰਿ ਵੇਖੈ ਕੀਤਾ ਆਪਣਾ ਜਿਵ ਤਿਸ ਦੀ ਵਡਿਆਈ ॥
Kar Kar Vaekhai Ketaa Aapana Jiv Tis Dhee Vadiaee.
HE creates and also watches over the virtuous.

ਜੋ ਤਿਸੁ ਭਾਵੈ ਸੋਈ ਕਰਸੀ ਹੁਕਮੁ ਨ ਕਰਣਾ ਜਾਈ ॥

Jap Meditation Revealed

Jo Tis Bhaavai Soee Karasee Hukam N Karanaa Jaaee.
HE does whatever pleases. No order can be issued to HIM.

ਸੋ ਪਾਤਿਸਾਹੁ ਸਾਹਾ ਪਾਤਿਸਾਹਿਬੁ ਨਾਨਕ ਰਹਣੁ ਰਜਾਈ ॥੨੭॥
So Paatsah Sahaa Pathsahib Nanak Rehan Rajaee.
HE is the King, King of Kings, Supreme Master of Kings Says Nanak, we should live in acceptance.||27||

Comments:

It is a fascinating description of ways in which worship is being done and the mythical stories woven around these.

We tend to follow the crowds doing visible rituals. Whereas the Guru asks us to be in acceptance (Raza).

The Raza means to align, to accept. This acceptance happens when we keep our awareness in Nirgun. This is an attitude with resentment giving way to understanding which comes of awareness of underlying singularity of origin.

The same light shines in all. The apparent diversity in appearance is the world play.

The Pauri need to be repeated and contemplated again and again as Jap, till *Nadar* (vision) is received.

Pauri 28

ਮੁੰਦਾ ਸੰਤੋਖੁ ਸਰਮੁ ਪਤੁ ਝੋਲੀ ਧਿਆਨ ਕੀ ਕਰਹਿ ਬਿਭੂਤਿ ॥
Mundaa Santokh Saram Patt Jholee Dhhyan Kee Karehi Bibhooth.
Make contentment the ear-rings, humility the begging bowl, and meditation the ashes that are applied to the body.

ਖਿੰਥਾ ਕਾਲੁ ਕੁਆਰੀ ਕਾਇਆ ਜੁਗਤਿ ਡੰਡਾ ਪਰਤੀਤਿ ॥
Khintha Kaal Kuare Kaeia Jugat Danda Parteet.
Let the remembrance of death be the patched coat, and keeping your mind away from vices be the purity of the body and let faith be the walking stick.

ਆਈ ਪੰਥੀ ਸਗਲ ਜਮਾਤੀ ਮਨਿ ਜੀਤੈ ਜਗੁ ਜੀਤੁ ॥
Aaee Panthe Sagal Jamaatee Man Jeethai Jag Jeet.
Know the right Aye Panthees (a higher sect of Yogis) is to conquer the mind which is to conquer the world.

ਆਦੇਸੁ ਤਿਸੈ ਆਦੇਸੁ ॥
Aadhaes Thisai Aadhaes.
Ever bow to HIM alone, always.

ਆਦਿ ਅਨੀਲੁ ਅਨਾਦਿ ਅਨਾਹਤਿ ਜੁਗੁ ਜੁਗੁ ਏਕੋ ਵੇਸੁ ॥੨੮॥
Aadh Aneel Anadh Anahat Jug Jug Eaeko Vaes ||28||
The Primal ONE, is without beginning, without end, eternal, is Same in all ages. ||28||

Comments:

The "Aaee Panth" was a famous sect of sadhus. They were ascetics. The ascetism looks attractive. The Guru does not approve of such an external display.

The Guru here mentions the correct way:
Earrings- Contentment.
Begging Bowl- Humility.

Ashes on body - Meditation.
Patched Coat - Remembrance of death.
Body purity - Mind away from vices.
Walking Stick - Faith.

The direction of Jap is to shift us away from duality. We easily get attracted by the "other ways" which have sargun elements: rituals, fastings, dancing, pilgrimage, adornments, offerings, sacrifices, austerities, penance. There are even strange practices. All are Maya's deception.

The Jap way takes us within, in the Nirgun world. Most of us refrain from Jap and Gurbani Vichar and expect to know about the Nirgun Naam. Within we are guided and handheld by none other than Satguru Purakh.

Who other is needed then?

Pauri 29

ਭੁਗਤਿ ਗਿਆਨੁ ਦਇਆ ਭੰਡਾਰਣਿ ਘਟਿ ਘਟਿ ਵਾਜਹਿ ਨਾਦ ॥
Bhugath Giaan Dhaeiaa Bhandharan Ghatt Ghatt VaajehiNaad.
The ONE is omnipresent, let this understanding be the food. The food serving be with compassion. And the awareness of life-creating presence of sound-current of the Naad vibrating in all beings be considered the conch sound.

ਆਪਿ ਨਾਥੁ ਨਾਥੀ ਸਭ ਜਾ ਕੀ ਰਿਧਿ ਸਿਧਿ ਅਵਰਾ ਸਾਦ ॥
Aap Naathh Naathhee Sabh Jaa Kee Ridhh Sidhh Avaraa Saadh.
The Nath (head) be Akal Purakh HIMSELF the Supreme Master of the universe; the pursuit of miraculous powers is an external taste.

ਸੰਜੋਗੁ ਵਿਜੋਗੁ ਦੁਇ ਕਾਰ ਚਲਾਵਹਿ ਲੇਖੇ ਆਵਹਿ ਭਾਗ ॥
Sanjog Vijog Dhue Kaar Chalaavehi Laekhae Aavehi Bhaag.
The awareness of Sanjog (uniting with Him), and Vijog (separation from Him) are the working in this world. We come to receive what we write as our destiny.

ਆਦੇਸੁ ਤਿਸੈ ਆਦੇਸੁ ॥
Aadhaes Thisai Aadhaes.
Ever bow to HIM alone, always.

ਆਦਿ ਅਨੀਲੁ ਅਨਾਦਿ ਅਨਾਹਤਿ ਜੁਗੁ ਜੁਗੁ ਏਕੋ ਵੇਸੁ ॥੨੯॥
Aadh Aneel Anaadh Anahat Jug Jug Eaeko Vaes.
The Primal ONE, without beginning, without end. Throughout all the ages, HE, the pure One is ever Same. ||29||

Comments:

The theme in this Pauri is continuation of previous Pauri. Here Guru is giving example of the practice of yogi's eating food as community serving to illustrate another significant hint.

Compassion in service of others as a way to develop humility.

Instead of the conch sound, the hearing of Naad be done by going within.

The Guru is emphasising another point about bowing to the Akal Purakh only. HE is Sach so is eternally same. We need to keep thinking about the Oneness and the presence of Sach. Rest is transient, created. The objects, possessions and the worldly affairs are sargun in nature.

With Gur Prashad from Satguru, the Sach comes to abide in the mind.

Pauri 30

ਏਕਾ ਮਾਈ ਜੁਗਤਿ ਵਿਆਈ ਤਿਨਿ ਚੇਲੇ ਪਰਵਾਣੁ ॥
Eaekaa Maaee Jugath Viaaee Thin Chaelae Paravaan.
The one Maya artfully married to the world has adopted three disciples.

ਇਕੁ ਸੰਸਾਰੀ ਇਕੁ ਭੰਡਾਰੀ ਇਕੁ ਲਾਏ ਦੀਬਾਣੁ ॥
Eik Sansaaree Eik Bhanddaaree Eik Laaeae Dheebaan.
Among these three forces one is worldly, the second one up-keeps as a Sustainer; and the third is that which Destroys.

ਜਿਵ ਤਿਸੁ ਭਾਵੈ ਤਿਵੈ ਚਲਾਵੈ ਜਿਵ ਹੋਵੈ ਫੁਰਮਾਣੁ ॥
Jiv This Bhaavai Thivai Chalaavai Jiv Hovai Furamaan.
The Creation happens as is HIS pleasure and the Hukam (Such is HIS Celestial Order).

ਓਹੁ ਵੇਖੈ ਓਨਾ ਨਦਰਿ ਨ ਆਵੈ ਬਹੁਤਾ ਏਹੁ ਵਿਡਾਣੁ ॥
Ouhu Vaekhai Ounaa Nadhar N Aavai Bahuthaa Eaehu Viddaan.
The Creator watches but is not seen; this is a great wonder.

ਆਦੇਸੁ ਤਿਸੈ ਆਦੇਸੁ ॥
Aadhaes Thisai Aadhaes.
Ever bow to HIM alone, always.

ਆਦਿ ਅਨੀਲੁ ਅਨਾਦਿ ਅਨਾਹਤਿ ਜੁਗੁ ਜੁਗੁ ਏਕੋ ਵੇਸੁ ॥੩੦॥
Aadh Aneel Anaadh Anaahath Jug Jug Eaeko Vaes ||30||
The Primal ONE, without beginning, without end. Throughout all the ages, HE, the pure One is ever Same. ||30||

Comments:

The ONE created Maya in creation. Its three forces are: Brahma, Vishnu and Mahesh which represent the forces giving

Birth, life sustainance and death. This cycle is characteristic about creation. What is born, grows or forms then lives leading next to decay or death.

In this creation the wonder of wonder is the hiddence presence of Sach. There is a prevailing thought that the Creation is an illusion. It is a dream.

The Guru however makes clear that the creation is real as it has presence of sach. The creation however is transcient and not eternally existing Sach. The creation is like an illusion. Also, it is like a dream. The Creation exists.

Pauri 31

ਆਸਣੁ ਲੋਇ ਲੋਇ ਭੰਡਾਰ ॥
Aasan Loe Loe Bhanddaar.
HIS seat of presence is in each and every person like a storehouse.

ਜੋ ਕਿਛੁ ਪਾਇਆ ਸੁ ਏਕਾ ਵਾਰ ॥
Jo Kishh Paaeiaa S Eaekaa Vaar.
Whatever is built as part of universe has been done once for all.

ਕਰਿ ਕਰਿ ਵੇਖੈ ਸਿਰਜਣਹਾਰੁ ॥
Kar Kar Vaekhai Sirajanehaar.
Having created the creation, the Creator Lord watches over it.

ਨਾਨਕ ਸਚੇ ਕੀ ਸਾਚੀ ਕਾਰ ॥
Nanak Sachae Kee Saachee Kaar.
Says Nanak, True is the Creator, and true is the Creation.

ਆਦੇਸੁ ਤਿਸੈ ਆਦੇਸੁ ॥
Aadhaes Thisai Aadhaes.
Ever bow to HIM alone, always.

ਆਦਿ ਅਨੀਲੁ ਅਨਾਦਿ ਅਨਾਹਤਿ ਜੁਗੁ ਜੁਗੁ ਏਕੋ ਵੇਸੁ ॥੩੧॥
Aadh Aneel Anaadh Anaahath Jug Jug Eaeko Vaes.
The Primal One, the Pure Light, without beginning, without end. Throughout all the ages, He is One and the Same. ||31||

Comments:

When did the creation started and what was before it started? The Guru explains that no one would know.

Creation has arisen from eternally existing presence without time which has created time.

The creation, the Guru says, is complete. Everything is placed there. The Nirgun (formless) and Sargun (form) exists in creation. Nirgun is potential state. The building blocks of form and system of worldly affairs, the cycles and the opposite pairs that let the creation flow are all in place because of Nirgun.

The building blocks of creation whether past, present or future come into creation with appearance of Duality at the same time. The Creation is complete all the time. Maya is the name for the whole process. The process of Maya lets creation be in place with ever part of creation having its Root in Sach.

The Jap takes the mind away from the idea of separate existence to oneness. Jap lets one perceive Sach within. With Jap the mind perceives the Sach presence in creation when awareness is kept within but eyes are open.

Pauri 32

ਇਕ ਦੂ ਜੀਭੌ ਲਖ ਹੋਹਿ ਲਖ ਹੋਵਹਿ ਲਖ ਵੀਸ ॥
Eik Dhoo Jeebha Lakh Hohi Lakh Hovehi Lakh Vees.
If one had 100,000 tongues, and these were then multiplied twenty times more, with each tongue;

ਲਖੁ ਲਖੁ ਗੇੜਾ ਆਖੀਅਹਿ ਏਕੁ ਨਾਮੁ ਜਗਦੀਸ ॥
Lakh Lakh Gaerraa Aakheeahi Eaek Naam Jagadhees.
he would repeat, hundreds of thousands of times, the Naam of the One, Lord of the Universe.

ਏਤੁ ਰਾਹਿ ਪਤਿ ਪਵੜੀਆ ਚੜੀਐ ਹੋਇ ਇਕੀਸ ॥
Eaeth Raahi Path Pavarreeaa Charreeai Hoe Eikees.
Following along this path, we climb the steps of the ladder, and come to be one from the thought of two (the other second).

ਸੁਣਿ ਗਲਾ ਆਕਾਸ ਕੀ ਕੀਟਾ ਆਈ ਰੀਸ ॥
Sun Galaa Aakaas Kee Keettaa Aaee Rees.
Hearing of the higher spiritual pursuits, even worms long to follow the path.

ਨਾਨਕ ਨਦਰੀ ਪਾਈਐ ਕੂੜੀ ਕੂੜੈ ਠੀਸ ॥੩੨॥
Nanak Nadharee Paaeeai Koorree Koorrai Thees.
Says Nanak, HE is known and met by way of the Nadar (vision of awareness). Otherwise the false (created) part of the world simply brings boastings of the false. ||32||

Comments:

Here in this Pauri is explained the method of Naam Jap. The purpose being to move from the thought patten of Duality to ONE. The word "eikees" means 21. Thus, from two to one.

The separate thinking is by haume. The moment we move within then we detach from fear and anxiety. Next to to shift haume based thoughts that connect with a self identity to attributing "ownership" meaning to the Creator. Our efforts bring Nadar - the conscious awareness perception. Then the understanding happens.

The Nadar brings perception of Sach.

The Jap changes our attitude also. We do not consider all things as belonging to us. Thus, there is no attachment to give rise to any suffering. There is no pain of loss nor pride of ownership. There is just joy of experience.

Pauri 33

ਆਖਣਿ ਜੋਰੁ ਚੁਪੈ ਨਹ ਜੋਰੁ ॥
Aakhan Jor Chupai Neh Jor.
We have no power to speak, neither any power to keep silent.

ਜੋਰੁ ਨ ਮੰਗਣਿ ਦੇਣਿ ਨ ਜੋਰੁ ॥
Jor N Mangan Dhaen N Jor.
We have no power to ask, neither any power to give.

ਜੋਰੁ ਨ ਜੀਵਣਿ ਮਰਣਿ ਨਹ ਜੋਰੁ ॥
Jor N Jeevan Maran Neh Jor. We have no power to live, neither any power to die.

ਜੋਰੁ ਨ ਰਾਜਿ ਮਾਲਿ ਮਨਿ ਸੋਰੁ ॥
Jor N Raaj Maal Man Sor. We have no power to become a ruler, about which after obtaining we become mentally feel important.

ਜੋਰੁ ਨ ਸੁਰਤੀ ਗਿਆਨਿ ਵੀਚਾਰਿ ॥
Jor N Surathee Giaan Veechaar. We have no power to have spiritual awareness, understanding and to contemplate.

ਜੋਰੁ ਨ ਜੁਗਤੀ ਛੁਟੈ ਸੰਸਾਰੁ ॥
Jor N Jugathee Shhuttai Sansaar.
We have no power even to find the way to escape from birth and rebirth.

ਜਿਸੁ ਹਥਿ ਜੋਰੁ ਕਰਿ ਵੇਖੈ ਸੋਇ ॥
Jis Hathh Jor Kar Vaekhai Soe. In His hand alone is the Power. Making all function He watches.

ਨਾਨਕ ਉਤਮੁ ਨੀਚੁ ਨ ਕੋਇ ॥੩੩॥
Nanak Outham Neech N Koe.
Says Nanak, no one is high or low. ||33|

Comments:

In this Pauri there is an emphasis on "Jor" which has been translated as power but it also fully means "no personal power of the self". We think that we have a power to run the body, to think, to take action. But reality is that this also belongs to Karta (Creator).

What ever that is happening in this world is the Hukam and would not be there without the presence of Sach. As we would see in the last chapter, the conscious awareness is not ours. Haume thinks all belong to us but reality is different.

The above Pauri is to be contemplated to let go of Haume. This state is called *"Jeevat Marna"*- to die while living. Here what dies is *Haume* and its idea of a separate self-identity. Such a state comes through *Simran meditation.* We can shed haume by repetitive remembrance that our consciousness is actually that of the *Karta Purakh*. In all Creation there is presence of only *Ekankar*. The apparent separatness in the physical world is Created Duality- the second other which is transcient non-permanence.

Pauri 34

ਰਾਤੀ ਰੁਤੀ ਥਿਤੀ ਵਾਰ ॥
Raatee Ruthee Thhithee Vaar.
The night, day, the date and the days.

ਪਵਣ ਪਾਣੀ ਅਗਨੀ ਪਾਤਾਲ ॥
Pavan Paanee Aganee Paathaal.
And the wind, water, fire and the Paatal (subtle regions.)

ਤਿਸੁ ਵਿਚਿ ਧਰਤੀ ਥਾਪਿ ਰਖੀ ਧਰਮ ਸਾਲ ॥
Tis Vich Dharti Thaap Rakhee Dharam Saal. In the midst of these, is established the earth as a home for Dharma.

ਤਿਸੁ ਵਿਚਿ ਜੀਅ ਜੁਗਤਿ ਕੇ ਰੰਗ ॥
Tis Vich Jeea Jugath Kae Rang.
Upon it, are placed the various species of beings.

ਤਿਨ ਕੇ ਨਾਮ ਅਨੇਕ ਅਨੰਤ ॥
Tinn Kae Naam Anaek Ananth. Their names are vast and endless.

ਕਰਮੀ ਕਰਮੀ ਹੋਇ ਵੀਚਾਰੁ ॥
Karamee Karamee Hoe Veechaar.
They are judged by the deeds and their actions, and are thus judged.

ਸਚਾ ਆਪਿ ਸਚਾ ਦਰਬਾਰੁ ॥
Sachaa Aap Sachaa Dharabaar.
True is Himself and True is His Court.

ਤਿਥੈ ਸੋਹਨਿ ਪੰਚ ਪਰਵਾਣੁ ॥
Thiththai Sohan Panch Paravaan.
There, look beautiful become pure removing five vices so get approved.

ਨਦਰੀ ਕਰਮਿ ਪਵੈ ਨੀਸਾਣੁ ॥
Nadharee Karam Pavai Neesaan.
The indicative signs are known through Nadar (vision of awareness) by karma.

ਕਚ ਪਕਾਈ ਓਥੈ ਪਾਇ ॥
Kach Pakaaee Outhhai Paae.
When the unripe is ripe, they get to obtain.

ਨਾਨਕ ਗਇਆ ਜਾਪੈ ਜਾਇ ॥੩੪॥
Nanak Gaeiaa Jaapai Jaae.
Says Nanak, when you go home, you will see this.
||34||

Comments:

This Pauri in a straight forward way tells the how earth is a *Dharam sal* - a place where Karmic Righteousness is judged from action.

The purpose of Dharma is achiement of purity. Thereafter the Nadar is received which is blessed by Satguru only.

Pauri 35

ਧਰਮ ਖੰਡ ਕਾ ਏਹੋ ਧਰਮੁ ॥
Dharam Khand Kaa Eaeho Dharam.
The is righteous living on earth is the khand of Dharma.

ਗਿਆਨ ਖੰਡ ਕਾ ਆਖਹੁ ਕਰਮੁ ॥
Giyan Khand Kaa Aakho Karam. The next is Gyan Khand (the knowledge awareness) of the Karma.

ਕੇਤੇ ਪਵਣ ਪਾਣੀ ਵੈਸੰਤਰ ਕੇਤੇ ਕਾਨ ਮਹੇਸ ॥
Kaethae Pavan Panee Vaisantar Kaethae Kaan Mehesh. In the creation the karma of many is worship of the wind, water and fire; and many worship Krishna and Shivas.

ਕੇਤੇ ਬਰਮੇ ਘਾੜਤਿ ਘੜੀਅਹਿ ਰੂਪ ਰੰਗ ਕੇ ਵੇਸ ॥
Kaethae Baramae Gharith Ghareah Roop Rang Kae Vaes. So many worship Brahma, the God that fashions forms of great beauty, adorned and dressed in many colours.

ਕੇਤੀਆ ਕਰਮ ਭੂਮੀ ਮੇਰ ਕੇਤੇ ਕੇਤੇ ਧੂ ਉਪਦੇਸ ॥
Kaetheeaa Karam Bhoome Maer Kaethae Kaethae Dhhoo Updesh.
So many are involved in karma guided by many kinds of preaching.

ਕੇਤੇ ਇੰਦ ਚੰਦ ਸੂਰ ਕੇਤੇ ਕੇਤੇ ਮੰਡਲ ਦੇਸ ॥
Kaethae Indh Chandh Soor Kaethae Kaethae Mandal Dhesh.
In the creation there are so many Indras, so many moons and suns, so many worlds and lands.

ਕੇਤੇ ਸਿਧ ਬੁਧ ਨਾਥ ਕੇਤੇ ਕੇਤੇ ਦੇਵੀ ਵੇਸ ॥
Kaethae Sidhh Budhh Naathh Kaethae Kaethae Dhaevee Vaes.
There are so many Siddhas and Buddhas, so many Yogic masters. So many Goddesses of various kinds.

ਕੇਤੇ ਦੇਵ ਦਾਨਵ ਮੁਨਿ ਕੇਤੇ ਕੇਤੇ ਰਤਨ ਸਮੁੰਦ ॥
Kaethae Dhaev Dhaanav Mun Kaethae Kaethae Rathan Samundh. There are so many demi-gods and demons, so many silent sages. So many jewels and oceans.

ਕੇਤੀਆ ਖਾਣੀ ਕੇਤੀਆ ਬਾਣੀ ਕੇਤੇ ਪਾਤ ਨਰਿੰਦ ॥
Kaetheeaa Khaanee Kaetheeaa Baanee Kaethae Paath Narindh. There are so many kinds of life, so many languages and so many dynasties of rulers.

ਕੇਤੀਆ ਸੁਰਤੀ ਸੇਵਕ ਕੇਤੇ ਨਾਨਕ ਅੰਤੁ ਨ ਅੰਤੁ ॥੩੫॥
Kaethea Surtee Sevak Kaethae Nanak Anth N Anth.
There are many Surti Sevaks (devotees who have their conscious awareness focussed through Jap on Sach), says Nanak, there is no end to the worship and worshipers. ||35|

Comments:

After telling the purpose of Earth life the Guru in this Pauri is revealing a secret by talking about Dharam Khand. The Khand means a part of whole. The Khand is neither a realm, a level or a stage.

It is in fact part of consciousness. Our conscious awareness is restricted by divisio n between conscious and the subconscious. In our worldly life we live with conscious awareness of Dharam Khand.

As Nadar is blessed by the Guru the other Khands of our awareness lets us perceive aspects of the Sach hitherto hidden.

The Gyan khand is opening up of our awareness to the right Karma.

This is Jap Meditation which has been indicated by usage of

the word *Surti Sevak* - those who are using conscious awareness (surt) with focus on Shabad (First focus on Gurbani hymns and when within then focus on Anhad Shabad).

The Pauri describes the karmic worship practices of many and in the last line is the Shabad Surt Jap meditation is indicated.

The Khands are closely connected with Nadar. Our perception changes. There is a Shabad (hymn) in Guru Granth Sahib on Ang-561 of Guru RamDas which tells the changes brought about the Nadar.

Pauri 36

ਗਿਆਨ ਖੰਡ ਮਹਿ ਗਿਆਨੁ ਪਰਚੰਡੁ ॥
Gyan Khand Meh Giyan Parchand.
In the Khand of Gyan (knowledge), the awareness reigns supreme.

ਤਿਥੈ ਨਾਦ ਬਿਨੋਦ ਕੋਡ ਅਨੰਦੁ ॥
Thithhai Naadh Binodh Kodd Anandh.
Within vibrates the Sound of the Naad, many feelings of bliss.

ਸਰਮ ਖੰਡ ਕੀ ਬਾਣੀ ਰੂਪੁ ॥
Saram Khand Kee Baanee Roop.
In the *Saram Khand* the language is that related to form.

ਤਿਥੈ ਘਾੜਤਿ ਘੜੀਐ ਬਹੁਤੁ ਅਨੂਪੁ ॥
Tithai Gharith Gharei Bahut Anoop. what in this Khand is made and fashioned is amazing.

ਤਾ ਕੀਆ ਗਲਾ ਕਥੀਆ ਨਾ ਜਾਹਿ ॥
Taa Keeaa Galaa Kathheeaa Naa Jaahi. The happenings of this Khand cannot be described.

ਜੇ ਕੋ ਕਹੈ ਪਿਛੈ ਪਛੁਤਾਇ ॥
Jae Ko Kehai Pishhai Pashhuthaae. One who tries to speak of these shall regret the incomplete attempt.

ਤਿਥੈ ਘੜੀਐ ਸੁਰਤਿ ਮਤਿ ਮਨਿ ਬੁਧਿ ॥
Tithai Ghareai Surat Matt Mann Budh. In this Khand are fashioned the conscious attention, intuitive, intellect and understanding of the mind.

ਤਿਥੈ ਘੜੀਐ ਸੁਰਾ ਸਿਧਾ ਕੀ ਸੁਧਿ ॥੩੬॥
Tithai Gharea Sura Sidha Kee Sudh.
In this Khand are fashioned the consciousness awareness which becomes aware of purity. ||36||

Comments:

The Gyan Khand attaches us with Satguru. First in the Gurbani we learn that:

ਸਭਿ ਕਰਮ ਧਰਮ ਹਰਿ ਨਾਮੁ ਜਪਾਹਾ ॥

All good karma and righteous living are found in Naam Jap. (Guru Granth Sahib- Ang:699).

Next as we follow and go within in Nirgun our Jap is done to meet the *Satguru*. The Satguru is heard as a guiding voice. There is even a dialogue. Mainly a feeling of presence and peace.

We also hear the Naad. This is to be heard while keeping awareness attached with it. This is Simran. In the *Saram Khand*, the intellect and Surt (conscious awareness) gets perceptive. The mind gives up mera-tera (mine and yours).

This weakens hold of Maya. In *Saram Khand* the focus is also on *Haume*. Jap is done to shed Haume. As we identify away from its world the awareness then perceives presence of Karta Purakh.

Jap Meditation Revealed

Pauri 37

ਕਰਮ ਖੰਡ ਕੀ ਬਾਣੀ ਜੋਰੁ ॥
Karam Khand Kee Baanee Jor.
In the Khand of Karma, the language is of "Joining together".

ਤਿਥੈ ਹੋਰੁ ਨ ਕੋਈ ਹੋਰੁ ॥
Thithhai Hor N Koee Hor.
No one else (other than those aware) dwells here,

ਤਿਥੈ ਜੋਧ ਮਹਾਬਲ ਸੂਰ ॥
Thithhai Jodhh Mehaabal Soor.
Here in Karam Khand, are the real braves persons who are spiritual heroes.

ਤਿਨ ਮਹਿ ਰਾਮੁ ਰਹਿਆ ਭਰਪੂਰ ॥
Tinn Mehi Raam Rehiaa Bharapoor.
In these persons is Ram (The Creators presence) in full awareness.

ਤਿਥੈ ਸੀਤੋ ਸੀਤਾ ਮਹਿਮਾ ਮਾਹਿ ॥
Tithai Setho Sethaa Mehimaa Maahi.
They are sewed with the presence of Akal Purakh in glorious admiration.

ਤਾ ਕੇ ਰੂਪ ਨ ਕਥਨੇ ਜਾਹਿ ॥
Taa Kae Roop N Kathanae Jaahi.
Their beautiful inner transformation cannot be described.

ਨਾ ਓਹਿ ਮਰਹਿ ਨ ਠਾਗੇ ਜਾਹਿ ॥
Naa Ouhi Marehi N Thaagae Jaahi.
They do not die (are Akal) nor deceived by the Maya.

ਜਿਨ ਕੈ ਰਾਮੁ ਵਸੈ ਮਨ ਮਾਹਿ ॥
Jin Kai Raam Vasai Man Maahi.
Within whose minds the Ram (*Karta Purakh*) abides.

103

ਤਿਥੈ ਭਗਤ ਵਸਹਿ ਕੇ ਲੋਅ ॥
Thithhai Bhagath Vasehi Kae Loa.
In this Khand devotees from many worlds dwell.

ਕਰਹਿ ਅਨੰਦੁ ਸਚਾ ਮਨਿ ਸੋਇ ॥
Karehi Anandh Sachaa Man Soe.
They are in joy; with minds imbued with the Sach, the true one.

ਸਚ ਖੰਡਿ ਵਸੈ ਨਿਰੰਕਾਰੁ ॥
Sach Khand Vasai Nirankaar. In the realm of Sach Khand, the Formless Lord abides.

ਕਰਿ ਕਰਿ ਵੇਖੈ ਨਦਰਿ ਨਿਹਾਲ ॥
Kar Kar Vaekhai Nadhar Nihaal.
The Sacha (Creator) sees to the created persons by bestowing them with Nadar, the spiritual bliss.

ਤਿਥੈ ਖੰਡ ਮੰਡਲ ਵਰਭੰਡ ॥
Thithhai Khand Mandal Varabhandd.
In Creation are innumerable planets, solar systems, galaxies.

ਜੇ ਕੋ ਕਥੈ ਤ ਅੰਤ ਨ ਅੰਤ ॥
Jae Ko Kathai Taa Anth N Anth.
When spoken these are found to be endless with no limit.

ਤਿਥੈ ਲੋਅ ਲੋਅ ਆਕਾਰ ॥
Thithhai Loa Loa Aakaar.
There are worlds upon worlds with many diverse forms in Creation.

ਜਿਵ ਜਿਵ ਹੁਕਮੁ ਤਿਵੈ ਤਿਵ ਕਾਰ ॥
Jiv Jiv Hukam Thivai Thiv Kaar.
As is the Hukam (commands), so do they live.

ਵੇਖੈ ਵਿਗਸੈ ਕਰਿ ਵੀਚਾਰੁ ॥ Vaekhai Vigasai Kar Veechaar.
Watching over all Creation HE rejoices, let us contemplate this.

ਨਾਨਕ ਕਥਨਾ ਕਰੜਾ ਸਾਰੁ ॥੩੭॥
Nanak Kathhanaa Kararraa Saar.
Says Nanak, to describe this is very hard. ||37||

Comments:

The Khands open only With Satgur's Nadar. The Jap is a call to Satguru. Our past has no relevance, what we are now is important. Our Awareness is Akal.

The search for the place of the ONE who has given rise to the Creation ends with finding HIM within and in all Creation. HE is all there is.

<u>**Jap Meditation Flow through Nadar,**
opening up of Conscious awareness (Surt)</u>

Dharam Khand
(Karma Experience, Birth Cycles)
Good Karma brings Nadar
Gyan Khand
(Meets Guru Guide; insightful knowledge)
Jap meditation to meet the Satguru Presence
Shram Khand
(Gives up Mera-Tera (Mine-Yours), attachments)
Jap Meditation to die to Haume by identifying with Karta.
Hears Anhad Shabad at Nirgun Point
Karam Khand
(Feels Hazuri (presence), Has control over five passions)
Jap Meditation on Charan Kamal for opening of Tenth Door.
Sach Khand
(Opening of tenth Door; Illuminated within, Anand)
Jap Meditation for Sehej; Jyote of Karta instead of Haume.

Pauri 38

ਜਤੁ ਪਾਹਾਰਾ ਧੀਰਜੁ ਸੁਨਿਆਰੁ ॥
Jath Paahaaraa Dhheeraj Suniaar.
Let self-control be the furnace, and patience the goldsmith.

ਅਹਰਣਿ ਮਤਿ ਵੇਦੁ ਹਥੀਆਰੁ ॥
Aharan Math Vaedh Hathheeaar.
Let understanding be the anvil, and spiritual wisdom the tools.

ਭਉ ਖਲਾ ਅਗਨਿ ਤਪ ਤਾਉ ॥
Bho Khalaa Agan Thap Thaao.
With the fear of obedience be the bellows, fan the flames of that be tapa (dedicated meditation).

ਭਾਂਡਾ ਭਾਉ ਅੰਮ੍ਰਿਤੁ ਤਿਤੁ ਢਾਲਿ ॥
Bhaanddaa Bhaao Amrit Thit Dhaal.
In the crucible of love, melt the Nectar (of Naam).

ਘੜੀਐ ਸਬਦੁ ਸਚੀ ਟਕਸਾਲ ॥
Ghareeai Shabad Sachee Taksaal.
And fashion with the Shabad, in this mint of truth.

ਜਿਨ ਕਉ ਨਦਰਿ ਕਰਮੁ ਤਿਨ ਕਾਰ ॥ ਨਾਨਕ ਨਦਰੀ ਨਦਰਿ ਨਿਹਾਲ ॥੩੮॥
Jin Ko Nadar Karam Thin Kaar. Nanak Nadharee Nadhar Nihaal.
As is the karma, so is the Nadar bestowed.
Says Nanak, with Nadar, the devotee is in bliss. ||38||

Comments:

In this last Pauri is summary. The example taken is that of Goldsmith tools using which gold is melted to make beautiful jewellery.

Instead of Gold it is the persons mind that is fashioned

through the Shabad in the mint furnace of Truth.

Self-control over five to be exercised repeatedly.

Spiritual wisdom from the Gurbani though contemplation.

Obediance by keeping in mind the respectful fear.

Loving feeling with awareness within during Jap.

The Shabad is heard within which is the place of Truth-Nirgun.

The ones who receive Nadar (vision) then are in bliss.

5. ਸਲੋਕੁ ॥ Salok

ਪਵਣੁ ਗੁਰੂ ਪਾਣੀ ਪਿਤਾ ਮਾਤਾ ਧਰਤਿ ਮਹਤੁ ॥
Pavan Guru Paane Pitaa Mata Dharath Mehat.
Air is the Guru, Water is the Father, and Earth is the Great Mother of all.

ਦਿਵਸੁ ਰਾਤਿ ਦੁਇ ਦਾਈ ਦਾਇਆ ਖੇਲੈ ਸਗਲ ਜਗਤੁ ॥
Dhivas Raath Dhue Dhaaee Dhaaeiaa Khaelai Sagal Jagath.
Day and night are the two nurses, in whose lap all the world is at play.

ਚੰਗਿਆਈਆ ਬੁਰਿਆਈਆ ਵਾਚੈ ਧਰਮੁ ਹਦੂਰਿ ॥
Changiaea Buriaeaa Vaachai Dharam Hadoor.
Good deeds and bad deeds-the record is ever watched and recorded by the mythical Lord of Dharma

ਕਰਮੀ ਆਪੋ ਆਪਣੀ ਕੇ ਨੇੜੈ ਕੇ ਦੂਰਿ ॥
Karme Aapo Aapanee Kae Naerai Kae Dhoor. According to their own actions, some are drawn closer, and some are driven farther away.

ਜਿਨੀ ਨਾਮੁ ਧਿਆਇਆ ਗਏ ਮਸਕਤਿ ਘਾਲਿ ॥
Jinee Naam Dhhiaaeiaa Geae Masakath Ghaal. Those who have meditated on the Naam (the Sach) depart after having done the hard effort.

ਨਾਨਕ ਤੇ ਮੁਖ ਉਜਲੇ ਕੇਤੀ ਛੁਟੀ ਨਾਲਿ ॥੧॥
Nanak Tae Mukh Oujalae Kaetee Chuttee Naal.
Says Nanak, their faces are radiant and are liberated from life - death karmic cycle. ||1||

Comments:

This is the last *Salok* (verse). It has vital information.

First is Air is stated to be like the Guru, Water is the Father, and Earth is the Great Mother of all.

Air is our life, without it we would die. The Guru here is Satguru Purakh. We exist because of presence of Purakh. Our consciousness is not ours but of the Purakh.

The Haume (our identity giver) is just Maya's creation. It gives us identity for worldly life experience.

Air is our life, without it we would die. The Guru here is Satguru Purakh. We exist because of presence of Purakh. Our consciousness is not ours but of the Purakh.

The water and earth are father and mother making up the physical body. In the Physical world karma holds sway. We get results as are our thoughts. The way out is through the Guru guide.

This is what the system in the world is. There are enough wrong paths. The only true path is the "inner guidance" from the Satguru (True Guru).

The words in Japji have profound indications. These words not simply tell but point out the meanings.

The inner wisdom reveals the truth to free us from Haume. Then comes the awareness of the play of Hukam. We are then our Mool in conscious awareness. The face as the Gurbani says is radiant.

6. Jap Meditation Explained

One aspect of Jap is to "repeat". This repetition is not chanting. The repetition in chanting way is done so as to have concentration and thereafter the mind has become silent. The Jap of Gurbani is an extraordinary process that opens up consciousness. Jap changes our State of being by going across in the timeless state.

The process is indicated in the Mool Mantar which describes Jap as below:

॥ ਜਪੁ ॥ Jap

ਆਦਿ ਸਚੁ ਜੁਗਾਦਿ ਸਚੁ ॥ ਹੈ ਭੀ ਸਚੁ ਨਾਨਕ ਹੋਸੀ ਭੀ ਸਚੁ ॥੧॥
Aadh Sach Jugaadh Sach. Hai Bhee Sach
Nanak Hosee Bhee Sach.

The True ONE existed before any beginning,
True ONE exists thereafter,
True ONE is present in now and,
says Nanak, True ONE shall remains existing in the future.

These words are significant and indicate the Jap process. The hidden is explained via a diagram.

In the Aadh, meaning before beginning there is no creation as such no form but the Sach exists.

When there is Jugad, meaning after beginning then also there was same Sach. In the Hai Bhee, present and Hosee Bhee, future there is unchanging same Sach.

Jap Meditation Revealed

Aadh (Before beginning)	Jugad (After beginning)	Hai Bhee (The present Now)	Hosee Bhee (The future)
Sach	Sach	Sach	Sach

Figure 3: Sargun and Nirgun Sach

The first line of boxes represents the Creation having Linear Time and also forms. This is known as Sargun (pronounced sargunn). This word is made from the two roots 'sar' which means 'with' and 'gunn' which means 'form' or 'quality'. So, these two combined means "with physical form" or "with quality/attribute".

The chief quality of Sargun is duality. In this exist opposites as pairs. There is up-down, heavy-light, hot-cold. This pairing is a long list making for a comparison and differenciation. There is also duality- meaning it has hidden aspects of true reality. The world of form is under life cycle of birth and death.

The other world is Nirgun (pronounced nirgunn). It also has two roots 'nir' which means 'without' and 'gunn' which means 'material/physical form/attribute/quality'. So, the two combined means "without form" or "without qualities" that are connected with the physical material world.

When we close our eyes, then we encounter both Sargun and Nirgun. The first observation is of an ever flow of thoughts interlinked with our emotional state. This is Sargun link. The Nirgun is the Consciousness. As we detach from *Haume* then the Sach begins to be perceived.

The feeling of love is connected to Bliss and finds its origin from Sach. Our Conscious awareness is part of Sach which along with Haume makes for our individuality for living in this world. the Haume is a created aspect.

Gurmeet Singh

Jap Process:

Jap is a process. It starts with keeping awareness away from past and future to the present.

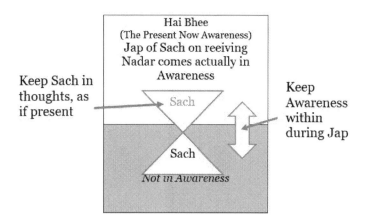

The focus point is "*thoughts about Sach*". These thoughts derived from the Mool Mantar. The Jap is to be done by keeping awareness (surt) within. Method to shift awareness within is by self-voicing and self-listening to Guru Mantra - Waheguru. Soon a pull is felt and thereafter it is easier to go within even when eyes are open.

The figure illustrates this in a simple way just representional to illustrate the point. When we do the Jap, Sach is not present is awareness but is hidden from perception. *Assume it is there. Do Jap with Sach as if present.* When Nadar is received, the Sach is actually observed to be present. The new awareness of Sach has to be in conscious awareness by being within by Simran. We have to keep the awareness focus by being within, with regularity.

The usage of words in Gurbani are purposeful. The Naam and Sach are same but purpose is different. Naam is for Jap and Simran. Many words that name the Ekankar in Gurbani are the Naam. The Mool Mantar describes Sach and is Naam. No single word is able to describes the reality. The Gurbani describes Sach and has originated from Sach.

Jap

The main basis of Jap is the Mool Mantar. The Gurbani further elaborates the Mool Mantar with indication towards understanding. The Khands of Japji Sahib are in a way stages in Jap.

Dharam Khand

Dharam khand is the beginning stage wherein our conscious awareness is involved in worldly life. Here our thoughts and actions are in Karmic Cycle. Through that we exercise choice and learn too.

Those with thirst for finding the path do get indications. The yearning and the prayers bear fruit. They receive the Nadar for Gyan (knowledge).

The Jap of Dharam Khand is listening to Shabad Kirtan or reading Gurbani lines in a poetic way again and again. The Mool mantar and the Pauries evoke love and peace. The Ardas (prayer) is done with feeling of being stanging surrounded by the Master, who always listens.

Gyan khand

Here Gyan is awareness of Sach. First, we like to go within. The Jap to take within is Gurumantar: "Waheguru".

The Gurumantar "Waheguru" is called an expression of wonder. When voiced and listened the awareness shifts within.

The Jap is to be done during early morning around 4.00 A.M. to 6 A.M which time is known as Ambroisal hour (Amritvela). The Sach to be contemplated on is presence of "Satguru".

Gurmeet Singh

The Satguru is the True Guru guide. We hear the voice within, can receive answer or remain in contemplative awareness of the Satguru presence within.

Do Simran meditation when within. During Simran do Jap of Gurumantar or be contemplative. Ask for hearing of Anhad Shabad - the ever-flowing Shabad, the Celestial Sound of Creation. This is heard at Charnarbind (pronounced Charnarbinnd).

It is the Nirgun point within, the location of which is shown in the diagram. This point is also called *"Pawan Bind"* in Gurbani indicating location.

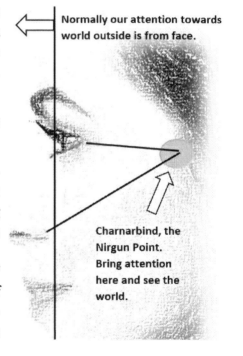

Figure 5- Charnarbind, the Nirgun point

At Nirgun point is heard the Anhad shabad and is also the point to keep the awareness during Simran or otherwise. Our eyes can be open or closed.
The Gyan received is of "formless" nature of the Creator. The Jap is of Akal Moorat, Ajooni and Saibhang. The self- existence does not need anything to exist.

The Akal Moorat is eternal existence.
The Akal quality is without any time or no time state. The Akal when in Nirgun is unaffected by the time state of Sargun.
In the Sargun there is "linear time flow".

The Sach presence is formless and perceptible when our

114

Jap Meditation Revealed

awareness is within.

Saram Khand

The Sach is Nirbhau, as such the "fear" is not part of Sach. The fear is a created and part of Sargun. In the Sargun is time with its past and future. There is also fear and anxiety. Inside the is peaceful state.

The Jap is of Nirbhau and Nirvair. The Sach with "no fear" has expression as Nirvair. There is just love. All Sargun existances arise due to Shabad and Hukam. The formless and the form is interlinked in creation. One is permanence while other is transient. One is limitless while other is limited. In one is the presence of Haume making for a separate identity. In the creation there is an unseen presence of Sach. This presence can be only felt.

When within then the grip of Maya and the five passions is less. These five are very strong in Sargun. But within Nirgun they are gone. the shift within is being with Naam, which is same as Sach but a broader word to indicate use of words that name the Sach to connect with the formless presence of Creator.

The Jap in this khand is awareness of the false nature of Haume. The "mera-tera" (mine -yours) begins to loose itself when within. The Jap is gives up mental associations of "mine". Keep Jap that these are "YOURS".

When Nadar comes, the grip of Haume is goes.

Karam Khand

The presence of Purakh is everywhere. When false Haume is not there then the reality is presence within of Karta Purakh.

The Jap is on nature of "Karta Purakh". The play of Hukam

is all round in the movement of creation. In the Creation is felt "Hazuri" - the presence of Sach. Simran is to keep seeing Hazuri within the "Mann-Tann" (Mind-Body) and also around in creation.

Within the body the Surt (awareness) keeps listening to the Anhad Shabad with Jap of "Charan Kamal". The word Charan means the "feet" which is the lowest body part. The formless Anhad Shabad is the lowest level gives rise to the five elements of creation. The Shabad is coming from the Crown chakra area.

The Chakras are opened by the Satguru. By now the Simran on Karta Purakh Hazur brings acceptance of the flimsy role of Haume in workings of Mind-Body as well. The Crown Chakra petals are opened by the Satguru. from above it the *Jyote* (light brilliance) lights up the whole body within.

Sach Khand

The Dasam Dwar (Tenth Door) on top of the head opens brining in awareness of *Sach*- Karta Purakh.
The Simran is then about Sehej (equipose) - detachment and peace.

This detachment is not of giving up but of non-involvement in Haume. The separateness of forms is perceived with awareness of oneness. The Simran is that of Hazuri.
Within is also Sunn, a state of Samadhi. The state where there is nothingness of creation. Where there is just the presence of Ekankar.

The Jap is a method where as Simran too is like Jap but is keeping the Sach in conscious awareness. The conscious awareness due to effect of Maya is enamoured by the Sargun charms. When the awareness is within in then the true charm is encountered. Simran is done while keeping awareness within with a regularity like that of breath. At very initial stages it is done along with breath but is soon dropped as breath has Sargun connection.

The way of Gurbani is of Nirgun. The rites, rituals, breath work etc are the ways having Sargun elements and not part of Jap Method.

The Head

The head and the mind encountered within are the working areas. The Mind is subtle and cannot said to be confined within head but has presence there. During Jap the top of the head is mostly hot due to movement of energies within.

Above the top of the Head is Dasam Dwar (tenth door). The Sikh Guru's did not cut the hairs and kept it covered by wearing turban. The Sikhs (disciples) likewise do not cut hair and cover head respecting the presence of Dasam Dwar (tenth Door).

From this spot the Anhad Shabad (Celistial Vibration of creation is heard as sound) is ever present. This Shabad is heard upto the Nirgun point where we are to keep our awareness.

This Nirgun is a place of Nirbhau and Nirvair - meaning there is no presence of fear and even resentment or anger of enmity. At this place is felt an awareness of Hazuri (the presence of Naam).

Japji and Healing

The Gurbani (Satguru's word) speaks of Mind-Body link in disease. Health of the body deteriorates when there is Haume's involvement with the five negative passions. The Japji composition when repeated takes on within and evokes a loving feeling of presence. Many have found healing through this Baani (composition).

7. The Jap and New Age

Gurbani has words which appear to be in usage by other religions for a long time. Among these are some new words in the Mool Mantar and elsewhere that bring in a comprehensive clarity. The Gurbani speaks in plain language and hides some clues which come out only on contemplation.

These words and concepts are contemporary in nature. The Jap meditation is for the shift needed to move into the "Fifth Dimensional" living.

The Jap takes one within the innerscape in the world of Nirgun, which is formless and timeless. The expression of Nirgun is Love.

The Nirgun is Nirbhau, having no presence of fear and Nirvair, having no feeling of resentment and enmity.

Within us is the Nirgun point (*Charnarbind*), where the awareness is to be kept when functioning in the physical world. At Nirgun Point we are free from fear and anxiety. We observe and feel as part of one whole.

The Soul element of Haume exists with links out in the physical world but within us is Karta Purakh conscious awareness. The awakened life is to live in Oneness.

8. About the Author

The author, as a humble service, has presented an English translation of "Japji Sahib" in this Book. This Baani (composition) has been brought to this world by Guru Nanak. *Author has been Guided and inspired by the Guru.* The book presents the insights given for Jap Meditation. The Method understanding has come from actual experience.

The author born to Sikh parents is a post graduate in science. He has lived a working life of a householder. Theis book is a part of the new spirituality initiated by Guru Nanak for the present era. The truths in Gurbani are meant to enlighten humanity towards living a life which is creative and with inner peace.

(contact: gurbaniguidance@gmail.com)

Manufactured by Amazon.ca
Bolton, ON